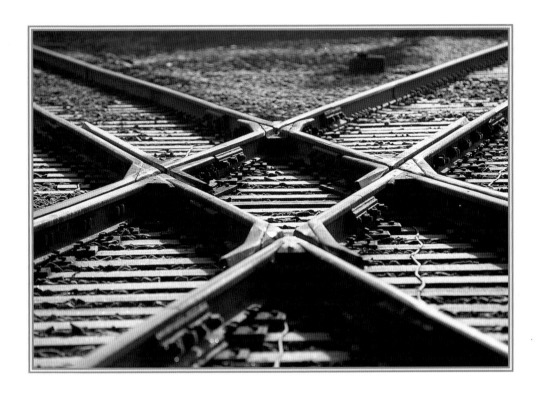

RAILWAY MAINTENANCE

The Men and Machines
That Keep the Railroads Running

Brian Solomon

MBI

Dedication

To my friends Mike and Linda Gardner

First published in 2001 by MBI, an imprint of MBI Publishing Company, Galtier Plaza, Suite 200, 380 Jackson Street, St. Paul, MN 55101-3885, USA.

MBI titles are also available at discounts in bulk quantity for industrial or sales-promotional use. For details write to Special Sales Manager at MBI Publishing Company, Galtier Plaza, Suite 200, 380 Jackson Street, St. Paul, MN 55101-3885, USA.

Library of Congress Cataloging-in-Publication Data Available

ISBN-13: 978-0-7603-0975-9
ISBN-10: 0-7603-0975-2

Edited by Josh Leventhal
Designed by Jim Snyder

About the Author: Brian Solomon is one of the most gifted talents in the train hobby today. He has authored many books on railroads, and his writings and photographs have been featured in the most popular rail-fan publications around the world, including *Trains, Railway Age, Passenger Train Journal,* and *RailNews.*

On the front cover: Southern Pacific's venerable rotary plows clear the tracks near Donner Pass during the severe winter of 1993.

Insets: A ballast regulator works the Wisconsin Central at Hawkins, Wisconsin, moving, sculpting, and manicuring ballast along the tracks.

In August 1988, Conrail's *Dirt Devil* undercutter churns away at Milepost 81 along the Boston & Albany.

On the back cover: A Loram grinder profiles Southern Pacific rails near Long Ravine at Colfax, California, in July 1990.

Gantry track-laying machines are often used to put new track down on railways overseas. The old track on a section of Iarnród Éireann (Irish Rail) near Glasnevin in Dublin has been removed, the sub-ballast prepared, and welded rail laid out for the gantry to run on. *Colm O'Callaghan*

On the frontis: Complicated track arrangements like this level "diamond" crossing have special maintenance requirements.

On the title page: Two Santa Fe GP7s shove a Jordan toward the Burlington Northern/Rock Island crossing at Dobbin, Texas, on August 3, 1981. *Tom Kline*

Printed in China

Contents

A few miles west of Pepin, Wisconsin, a steel gang is regauging rail with a Pettibone crane and a Kershaw Kribber-Adzer.

Preface and Acknowledgments

During the many years I have spent learning about railway operations and taking photographs, I have often encountered railway maintenance equipment, witnessing everything from switch tampers to rotary plows. While I've always made an attempt to photograph these machines, I hadn't thought of them as a distinct subject until discussing the concept with Steve Hendrickson at Motorbooks. When he asked if I would be interested in writing a book on railway maintenance, I said "Yes," without hesitation. When I agreed to write this book, I didn't realize how little I knew about the equipment and processes that I had been watching for so long. Researching this project has proved a great education for me. I could never claim to be an expert on railway maintenance, but I have learned an enormous amount about the subject, and it continues to capture my interest. Machines that seemed to have fairly simple functions turned out to be quite

Three pieces of track equipment work together surfacing track: a ballast regulator, a Mark IV production tamper, and a chase tamper.

complex. Subjects I would have dismissed as pedantic were actually very interesting.

This book is intended as an overview of railway maintenance and the men and equipment that make it happen. My intention is to share my interest in why maintenance is needed, how the equipment works, what it does, and what it looks like. When I felt it was appropriate, I included background information about the people who invented or designed equipment and maintenance processes, and a little bit of history about some of the manufacturers. Specific manufacturer's equipment is described to provide real-life examples of the different types of maintenance machines; it is not my intent to endorse one company's product over another's, nor do I intend to compare and contrast the virtues of different manufacturers. This text is not the forum for such critical analysis, and I have neither the level of expertise nor the interest to perform such a critique.

I could not have not have written this book without the help of many people, including industry professionals, representatives of equipment manufacturers, fellow photographers, and maintenance equipment enthusiasts. Some have helped me directly by explaining equipment operation or maintenance theory and practice, or by lending me photographs; others assisted indirectly in my quest for information and illustrations.

Thanks to: my father, Richard Jay Solomon; John and Bonnie Gruber; Dick Gruber and Paul Swanson of the Wisconsin & Southern Railroad; Dave Swirk and the maintenance crew of the Pioneer Valley Railroad; H. Bentley Crouch; Stephen Carlson; John Eagan; Doug Eisele; Tim Doherty; Colm O'Callaghan; Jim Shaughnessy; Dennis Lebeau; Robert A. Buck of Tucker's Hobbies; George C. Corey; George S. Pitarys; Howard Ande; Mike Schafer; Joe McMillan; Tom Hoover; Mel Patrick; Mark Hemphill; Dick Dorn; Richard Steinheimer; Brian Jennison; Tom Kline; Mike Abalos; and Pat Yough. Also thanks to MTA Metro-North Railroad's R. E. Lieblong, Chief Maintenance of Way Officer; J. L. Wagner, Director, Track and Structures; R. C. Kirner Jr. Assistant Director, Track Coordination; Doug Main at Sperry Rail Service; Roger Hendrickson and Bruce Goraczkowski of Harsco Track Technologies; the Irish Railway Records Society; Iarnród Éireann (Irish Rail); and Brian Moroney of Amtrak. Thanks also to maintenance crews on the Burlington Northern Santa Fe, Cartier Railway, Conrail, CSX, Southern Pacific, Union Pacific, and Wisconsin Central.

—Brian Solomon

Although much of the maintenance work is done by machines, such as this undercutter, which require far fewer people do to more work than traditional manual maintenance methods, a track gang is still needed to operate the machines and ensure the job is done properly.

Track

rack is a fundamental component of the railroad. The structure and function of tracks are fairly simple, but they must be clearly understood if we are to fully comprehend railway maintenance and the tasks required of railway maintenance equipment. Railroad track is designed to guide the train while evenly distributing its weight and providing adequate drainage. Track must be flexible and responsive to the effects of a variety of weather conditions. It must accomplish these functions as economically and as simply as possible, while remaining easy to maintain.

The guiding function of tracks is fairly obvious. The tracks provide a smooth, unbroken running surface. Wheels run on the rails and are held in place by the weight of the train, which puts vertical pressure on them. Flanges located on the inside dimension of the wheels prevent lateral movement beyond the track.

The tracks' function for weight distribution is less apparent, but equally important. It is easier to understand how weight transferal works if the whole track structure is viewed as a pyramid, starting with the rails on top, and working down through the different components in order of their placement: rails, tie plates, ties, ballast, sub-ballast, and sub-grade. Each component transfers and distributes the weight of the passing train over a greater area, beginning with the wheel-rail contact point and continuing all the way down to the sub-ballast and the ground below, known as the sub-grade. The failure of any of these components can result in the collapse of the track structure.

Monitoring the condition of the track and all its components is an essential part of effective railway maintenance.

Continuous welded rail adds a level of maintenance difficulty when a defect is located. The defective segment must be physically cut out and replaced with a new section. Welders use a portable welding kit to repair track on the Wisconsin Central at Camp Lake, Wisconsin, on October 27, 1999. *Howard Ande*

Track serves a number of important functions, not only guiding the train but also distributing its weight. A laden coal train, such as this one in Wyoming's Powder River basin, can weigh as much as 15,000 tons, so proper weight distribution is imperative. On the left, the newly laid track with continuous welded rail and concrete ties will need to be ballasted, aligned, and tamped before it is ready for traffic.

The railway inspectors must look for signs of defects that may reveal more serious problems. Railway maintenance aims to keep the track structure in shape to carry the load it is designed for.

Early History

The basic components of modern track were established more than 200 years ago in Britain by early tram lines, the primitive industrial railways. Over the years, the size and composition of the track components have evolved to reflect the development of more modern materials and the need to support ever faster and heavier trains. So while modern track has a common structure with tracks from the early railways, the materials used for track have changed.

Primitive tracks on British tram railways were composed of wooden rails set on wooden sleepers (known in America as crossties); some lines used stone blocks instead of wood. Sleepers rested on a crude sub-grade support that was often little more than bare earth. Strings of four-wheel tram carts were hauled along the tracks by horses or oxen. Originally the rails were flanged rather than the wheels. Later wheels were flanged, but initially the flange was on the outside rim of the wheel, rather than on the inside as they are today. Wheeled carts pulled on rails offered a more efficient way of hauling heavy loads than on conventional rutted roads. Animals could haul greater loads using a fixed track, which avoided problems of ruts and mud. In the early part of the nineteenth century, the first steam locomotives were built to supplement animal teams on tram railways. Since the engines were much heavier than loaded wagons, the track structure needed strengthening to accommodate them.

Track Gauge

Some early British tram lines used a 5-foot outside track width, or track gauge. The inside measurement of this track gauge was roughly 4 feet, 8.5 inches. (In the early days, the distance between the rails—known as track gauge—was measured from the outside distance between the rails; today we measure gauge as the inside distance between the rails.) In the early 1820s, railway pioneer George Stephenson adopted this width for his Stockton & Darlington line, the world's first steam-powered public railway. Stephenson's chosen gauge was subsequently adopted by most railway lines in Britain. Since early American railways took their cues from British practice, and frequently imported their locomotives from Britain, many early American lines also used the track gauge of 4 feet, 8.5 inches. There were many exceptions to this standard over the years, but the Stephenson Standard is now the most common gauge in Europe, America, and many countries around the world.

Track gauge is one of the few constants in railway practice, linking modern railways with the very earliest steam-powered lines. While just about everything else has changed, from the motive power to the way railroads operate, the track width remains the same. Some of the earliest preserved locomotives, such as the Robert Stephenson & Company's *Rocket*, built in 1829, or the *John Bull*, built in 1831, for export to the Camden & Amboy in New Jersey, could operate on modern tracks.

Track that isn't properly maintained gradually deteriorates to the point that trains have to operate extremely slowly to avoid derailment. This section of former Milwaukee Road near Kimball, South Dakota, is suffering from low joints, badly fouled ballast, and rotting ties. The track was still being used when this photo was taken in May 1995, albeit with a maximum track speed of 5 miles per hour.

Rail

Early rails were little more than wooden beams. The addition of thin iron straps nailed to the top of the rails was one of the first improvements designed to prolong the life of the rails and reduce the chance of their snapping under loads. The emergence of locomotives, even the small early machines built for tram lines, required heavier, more durable rails than those used strictly for animal-powered lines. Solid iron rails were developed that were safer and more durable than wooden strap-iron rails. In Britain, early steam railways employed several different types of heavy cast-iron rails. One of the most common was descriptively known as a "fish belly" for its distinctive shape; it was thin at the ends and fat in the middle. American railways were not as enthusiastic about these heavy cast-iron designs, partly because of the high cost of manufacturing and importing them from Britain.

In summer 2000, Wisconsin Central rehabilitated its Ladysmith Subdivision, replacing ties, adding ballast, and aligning track in conjunction with tamping. This track has just been worked over by a ballast regulator and is about to be aligned with a tamper.

In 1831, Camden & Amboy's Robert Stevens designed an improved style of iron rail that featured a profile resembling the letter "I" or an inverted "T," commonly known as the "Tee rail" because of its shape. This rail style has a broad thin base with a thin neck (sometimes described as a web) and a narrow-width thick head. The Tee rail was originally made from cast or wrought iron and could be easily produced domestically, making it popular with early lines in the United States. The Tee rail demonstrated durability, versatility, and cost effectiveness, and in the 170 years since it was introduced, it has become the most common style of rail in the world, replacing most other varieties. Though the Tee rail has undergone a variety of compositional changes, its essential structure remains basically unaltered.

The Tee rail is the standard rail design used throughout North America and the world. The basic profile of the Tee rail remains the same, but its size and weight can vary greatly depending on the type and quantity of traffic it is intended to support.

The early Tee rails made from iron were much smaller and lighter than those used today. Wrought-iron rails were brittle because of their high carbon content and were prone to snapping under heavy loads. During the last quarter of the nineteenth century, the introduction of inexpensive steel, manufactured by the Bessemer and open-hearth processes, allowed the production of relatively cheap steel rails. These were considerably more durable than rails fashioned from rolled iron. Today, rails are rolled from high-quality modern alloy steels and use much heavier profiles than the early rails, so they are significantly stronger and more malleable. The different elements that are alloyed to improve the characteristics of steel include manganese and vanadium. Since impurities in the steel will result in structural defects, it is important that rails are rolled from the highest quality steel, with minimal amounts of sulfur, phosphorous, and other undesirable elements. The proper rolling and cooling of rail is also crucial to minimizing structural defects. Improved processes for controlled steel cooling, developed in the 1930s, reduced the occurrence of rail defects.

Strict standards have been developed over the years to ensure good rail design and high production

The joint is one of the weakest parts of the track structure and is often the cause of continual maintenance headaches. This telephoto view at Cresson, Pennsylvania, illustrates the effect of low joints resulting from poor maintenance.

quality. In the United States, modern rails are described by their weight, cross section, and manufacturer. This information is imprinted at the rail ends, along with information on when and where it was rolled. Rail weight is measured in pounds per yard. Early rails weighed just 40 or 50 pounds per yard, and modern rail is manufactured in various weights between 80 and 150 pounds per yard. The weight and profile of rail is directly related to the type and amount of traffic it is designed to carry. By the turn of the nineteenth century, more than 120 different rail profiles had been developed that adhered to the basic Tee-rail design. Since that time different organizations, such as the American Society of Railway Engineers, have made efforts to standardize rail designs and limit the amount of variation.

Rail is a continuous smooth surface that must support the weight of the train rolling over it. With properly surfaced rail, the contact point between the wheel and the rail is only about the size of a dime. The rail distributes this weight downward through the track structure, and the profile and weight of the rail should match the type of train intended to operate on it. On a branch line that sees light, slow, or infrequent traffic, relatively light rail will suffice. A heavily used mainline, such as one that carries dozens of 13,000-ton coal trains daily operating at speeds up to 60 miles per hour, will require heavy rail, usually weighing 135 pounds per yard or more. Since heavier rail is more expensive, railroads try to match as closely as possible the type of rail with the intended service. The production and chemical composition also influence the type of rail used for different locations and purposes.

Traditional rail was manufactured in set lengths, usually 39 feet long, and connected with bolted joints. North American practice typically staggered the rail joints, which created the classic "clickety-clack" sound familiar to American railway passengers. Most railways overseas preferred parallel joints. Each system has its advantages and disadvantages. A 39-foot length is also easily transported on standard 40-foot-long flatcars.

Steel rails expand and contract with changes in temperature. Rail should be installed at warmer temperatures in order to avoid buckling, which can occur if rail is installed cold and then expands with increasing temperatures. Furthermore, space must be allowed at the joints to allow for some expansion. If the rail is installed and fastened properly, the overall structure of the track will tighten as the rail contracts in lower temperatures. If rail is installed cold and not secured properly, it will buckle as the temperature rises.

Old-fashioned jointed rail has largely given way to continuous welded rail, which usually

Modern track uses continuous welded rail and concrete ties. This type of track requires modern fasteners to hold the rail firmly to the tie. Here Union Pacific tracks catch the sun in Clover Creek Canyon, east of Caliente, Nevada.

comes in 1,500-foot-long sections. Welded rail has many advantages over jointed rail. The inherent unevenness of rail joints results in more wear to wheels and related components. The constant pounding of the wheels against the rail joints is also damaging to the rail ends and to the joints themselves. Eliminating the joints reduces maintenance and produces a smoother ride while minimizing wear to wheels and other equipment. Welded rail has its own set of problems, howev-

Lengths of continuous welded rail are transported on specially designed trains consisting of a string of flat cars with racks. Welded rail is flexible and can easily negotiate curves as the train rolls along. This Southern Pacific rail train was photographed at Troy, California, on Donner Pass in June 1994.

er. One of the primary difficulties with welded rail relates to the effects of expansion and contraction already discussed. During times of extreme temperature change, welded rail is more likely to develop serious heat kinks. In the most extreme circumstances, this will cause the rail to violently spring loose from the track structure. If this occurs below the wheels of a moving train, the results can be disastrous. Conversely, in times of extreme cold weather, rail shrinkage can lead to "pull aparts," where the rail sections actually separate from one another, leaving a sizable gap in the tracks. This dangerous situation can lead to a derailment.

These problems can be avoided by proper installation and by ensuring that there are sufficient fasteners to hold the rail in place. With proper fastening, expansion will occur in the rail width rather than the lengthwise expansion that can cause buckling. Rail is under its greatest tension on the outside of curves and is more likely to buckle on a curve than on straight sections of track, particularly curves located at the bottom of a grade. As a result, extra spikes, rail anchors, or fastening clips are needed to secure steeply curving track. Even with proper installation, regular track inspection to look for signs of weakness is key to avoiding major problems.

Another difficulty with welded rail has to do with routine maintenance. Jointed rail is relatively easy to adjust, replace, and repair, since the 39-foot-long sections can be replaced by a typical track gang of just a dozen or so men. Without need for complicated machinery, a track gang can lift these sections into place and spike them down fairly quickly. When a serious defect is found on a rail section, the section can easily be replaced with a new one. Such replacement is not as simple with welded rail, and even basic maintenance procedures are more involved. When a quarter-mile-long rail develops a crack or other defect, it is impractical to change the entire segment. Instead, the defective portion of rail must be cut out and a replacement piece welded or bolted in place. While such repairs are routine, they can take more time and effort than simply replacing a standard 39-foot section. The procedure for replacing welded rail is relatively complex, involving portable welding kits that use a flammable chemical compound.

Crossties

Crossties (usually described as simply "ties"), spikes, tie plates, and anchors are the track components that hold the rails in place and in gauge while they support the weight of the train. Like the rail itself, these components have gradually evolved into their modern form, yet have close historical connections to early track components. The days of the cut-stone sleeper have long since passed, and though wood has proven to be one

of the best and most versatile materials for railroad ties, it has been supplemented by other materials. Many different types of wood have been used for ties over the years, but treated hardwoods are now preferred for their stability, durability, and longevity.

In the 1930s, the American Railway Engineering Association listed 27 types of wood as suitable for use as railway ties. Among them were cherry, chestnut, elm, hemlock, hickory, oak, and walnut. A number of softwoods were also listed, including various pines, firs, and redwood. According to the fifth edition of the *Elements of Railroad Engineering*, between 1925 and 1934 the most common type of wood for ties was oak; roughly 199,163,190 oak ties were in use at that time in the United States, or 37 percent of all ties, which totaled 538,667,703 (give or take a few here and there). Southern pine accounted for 24.5 percent of all ties, and Douglas fir for 9.6 percent; all other

Many different types of wood can be used for crossties, although oak is generally preferred. A wooden tie ought to last for several decades. The tie serves to hold the rails in gauge while distributing the weight of the train.

after they were installed. By contrast, hardwood ties treated with creosote can have a remarkably long life, and some can last for more than 60 years. Creosote and pressure treatments are used to make ties water-resistant and to help retard decay.

Traditionally when ties were installed a date nail was placed in the ties to help the maintainers of the track gauge how long the ties were in service, and when they should be replaced. In later years, instead of the date nails, ties were branded with the date of installation. Although date nails have been out of fashion for decades, they can still be found on ties used for sidings, yard tracks, and secondary mainlines. A close inspection of track may reveal nails from the 1930s and 1940s and even earlier, which gives one an appreciation for how long wooden ties can last in daily service. Today, ties are mass-produced to predetermined specifications, finished on all sides, and treated to minimize decay and extend their service life. A new wooden tie appears nearly black and is remarkably uniform.

In recent times, reinforced concrete ties, and even steel ties and plastic ties have come into general use. Concrete ties are more expensive than wooden ties, but they are designed for long life under high-stress conditions. Tracks built with concrete ties offer greater stability, since concrete ties are significantly heavier than conventional wooden ties, weighing up to three times as much. Concrete ties are typically preferred on lines with very heavy tonnage like the coal lines in the Powder River Basin, and on high-speed routes, such as Amtrak's Northeast Corridor, and super fast lines in Europe and Japan.

Spikes, Tie Plates, and Anchors

Making sure that the rails are properly fastened to the ties is a very important consideration to ensure that tracks remain in gauge under varying degrees of stress. Traditionally rails were secured to wooden ties using track spikes. As the size and weight of rail has grown over the years, so has the size of the spikes. Spikes hold the rails to the ties and limit sideways movement. In the early days, rails were fastened directly to the ties, but today a tie plate made from rolled steel is placed between the rail and the tie. A tie plate is designed to seat the rail on the tie, while helping to spread the weight of the train and the rail over a larger area on the tie. This prolongs the useful life of the tie by minimizing wear, gives the rail additional support, and provides a sound base to spike the rail in place. A tie plate is wide and flat. Ideally the tie plate is broader on the field side to accommodate the great stress that is placed on the outside of the rail by the forces of a passing train. To further check these forces, the plate seat

types of wood constituted a much less significant portion of the total. Hardwood ties have good tension characteristics, which allow them to grip spikes well, yet they are sufficiently flexible to cushion the impact of a rolling train.

Early railroads used whatever kind of wood was available for ties. The ties were cut by hand and often left unfinished. Looking at photos of early tracks, it is interesting to note that the ties were sometimes little more than logs below the rails. They varied considerably in length and width, and sometimes even still had bits of bark on them. Untreated ties made from inferior types of wood, such as cottonwood, disintegrated quickly and needed replacement just a few years

This stack of surplus tie plates shows them in profile. A tie plate is designed to hold the rail in place, helps distribute the weight of the train over a broader area of the tie, and prolongs the life of the tie. When the tie plate is placed on the track, the larger side faces outward to provide greater support on the outside of the rail.

is angled slightly to position the rail inward toward the track center. The rail is seated between tapered shoulders, with a distinct lip designed to restrain lateral rail motion.

Typically a rail is seated on the tie plate and spiked in place with two to eight spikes placed in precut holes in the plate. The number of spikes used depends on a variety of considerations, including the position of the rail, the top speed of the trains, train frequency, and maximum weight. Rail located on the outside of a curve at the bottom of a heavily traveled mainline grade will require more spikes than on lightly used tangent track.

Augmenting the rail spike and tie plate is the rail anchor. This longitudinal clip is fastened to the base of the rail between and parallel to the ties to restrict the lengthwise motion of the rail. Without rail anchors, the rail would slide along the tie plates as a result of forces placed upon it by passing trains, as well as from the natural swelling and contraction caused by temperature fluctuations.

Some modern track designs use specially designed spring clip fasteners instead of traditional spikes and rail anchors. The most common of

these is manufactured by Pandrol. Known as the "Pandrol fastener," it resembles an enormous steel paper clip. These clips are attached to specially designed tie plates, which are held to wooden ties using large screws. A number of other modern fasteners are also used in place of spikes and rail anchors.

In addition to these fasteners, rail braces are applied to switches and sharp curves where abnormally high lateral forces are exerted against the rail. Normally braces are used just to support the outer rail in a curve, but they are sometimes placed on the inner rail as well. Braces are typically manufactured from either cast or pressed steel and held in place with spikes or track screws.

Tracks built using concrete ties have different fastening requirements than conventional track using wooden ties. Rail is attached to concrete ties with a special style of cliplike fastener that connects to steel plates cast into the tie. Cushioned pads are inserted between the rail and the tie. Since concrete ties are much stronger and heavier than wooden ties, they can be spaced further apart.

A maintenance gang prepares a section of track for tamping at Hawkins, Wisconsin. The two new ties on the track in the foreground are evidence that a tie gang has just been through. A little ballast has been spread over the tracks, but has not been attended to by a regulator.

Ballast, Sub-ballast, and Sub-grade

The ties on a railroad track are set into ballast, which has several important functions: First, ballast is integral to the track structure and keeps the ties in place, countering forces placed on the ties by rail expansion and passing trains. Secondly, ballast must support the track and distribute the load it carries from the tie bottoms. The force transferred from tie to ballast is considerable. John H. Armstrong indicates in his book, *The Railroad: What It Is, What It Does,* that under load, the average pressure below each tie is 100 psi. The third important function of ballast is to quickly and efficiently drain water away from the track structure, as standing water can rapidly damage tracks. Ballast also acts to keep down vegetation that might interfere with the track structure. Ballast must do all these things, yet also remain flexible and easy to work with, so that track repairs, such as tie and rail renewal and tamping, can be conducted with minimal difficulty.

Why is it called ballast anyway? Like so many specialized elements of railroad technology, railroad ballast derives its name from marine shipping. Traditionally, ballast referred to stones used to weigh down a ship.

A variety of materials have been used for railroad ballast over the years. The earliest lines ballasted tracks with earth and loose stones. During the mid-nineteenth century, cinders dumped from locomotive fireboxes served as typical ballast.

Today crushed stone is the most common ballast material, although the size and type of stone used by each railroad varies with availability and the nature of the lines. Gravel and crushed-stone ballast has the added advantage that it locks together, inhibiting track movement.

Ballast is placed between, below, and around the ties to keep them in place. The amount of ballast applied to a section of track varies, depending on the size and spacing of the ties, the amount of traffic expected over the line, whether the track is straight or curved, and other factors. A typical single-track tangent line has ballast laid even with the tops of the ties, extending 14 inches beyond either side of the ties on the level, then tapering off at a 3-to-1 slope extending up to 9 feet, 10 inches beyond the track center. The depth of this top ballast layer extends 1 foot below the bottom of the ties. Additional ballast beyond this is considered the sub-ballast and is treated as a separate track component.

The sub-ballast, typically small crushed stones, provides solid support for the top ballast. It also seals out water from the sub-grade to prevent it from saturating. The sub-grade is the layer below the sub-ballast, typically the earth and stones underneath the track. If the sub-grade becomes saturated with water, the pumping action caused by a passing train will rapidly undermine the structural integrity of the ballast, ties, and rail, causing long-term damage that can ultimately result in a derailment.

Pink Lady Quartz

Most large railroads would serve a quarry that provided stone ballast for the whole system. Often the tracks of a particular line could be identified by the type and color of ballast used. For example, the Chicago & North Western got most of its ballast from a quarry at Rock Springs, Wisconsin, that produced a rose-colored quartz called Pink Lady. All across the Midwest, C&NW's lines used Pink Lady ballast, which immediately distinguished its tracks from other railroads in the region. C&NW's relationship to the line that served the quarry illustrates the importance of good ballast to a railroad. Rock Springs was located on the Madison to Twin Cities mainline, for many years an important passenger line. In later years,

C&NW discontinued passenger service over this line, and ultimately re-routed freight trains operating between Chicago and the Twin Cities to other routes. It eventually abandoned the railroad west of the quarry, and this stub-end line was kept open primarily to provide the railroad with Pink Lady ballast. One factor in C&NW's decision to continue using this type of ballast, rather than finding another type of rock, was that this quartz was harder than most other types of ballast stone, and thus could not be mixed. Over time and with the constant passage of trains, the harder stone would grind up the softer stone. It was simply more practical to keep the line open than to replace the ballast on the entire railroad.

Detecting Track Defects

Santa Fe did everything in style; even its track geometry train had the appearance of a pocket streamliner. Spring is in the air, the grass is green, flowers are blooming, and Santa Fe is preparing for its maintenance season as its inspection train rolls westbound through Christie in California's Franklin Canyon.

Since rails both support and guide trains, they are one of the most crucial components of track structure. A railroad can survive with minor ballast problems, a few broken ties, missing spikes, and cracked tie plates, but a single rail failure can cause serious derailments and crashes. As railways progressed and trains became faster and heavier, the consequences of broken rails became an ever more serious issue. By 1900, the advent of powerful steam locomotive designs, air brakes, and automatic signaling systems permitted passenger trains to regularly operate at 80 miles per hour and faster. A derailment at such speeds can result in tremendous loss of life. Therefore, careful and thorough inspection of the tracks is essential for ensuring safe and reliable travel on the lines.

Traditionally, tracks and rails were inspected by expert track walkers, who regularly patrolled a section of line on foot, looking for defects. This inspection would reveal most flaws in the track structure, since many types of defects are detectable through close observation. A track inspector could easily spot potential problems in the ballast, ties, and fasteners. He would make note of any defects, and the section gangs would make the necessary repairs without risk to trains or passengers. Unfortunately, not all flaws are visible to the naked eye. Among the most serious of the invisible defects are tiny cracks inside the rail, particularly the trans-

The Federal Railroad Administration (FRA) plays a major role in inspecting and monitoring track conditions in the United States. The FRA's T-10 inspection car is shown here in a siding at Houston, Texas. The track is "blue flagged" to prevent unauthorized people from moving a train or equipment while it is being serviced. *Tom Kline*

dating safer operations. Federal laws required the use of air brakes, automatic knuckle couplers, steel-framed cars, and other safety equipment to help make trains safer to ride and work on. Unfortunately, safety initiatives were often acted upon only in the wake of a disaster. In 1902, a terrible crash was caused by a signal being obscured by heavy smoke in the Park Avenue Tunnel in New York City. The crash led to laws that forced railroads to electrify their New York passenger operations to eliminate smoke hazards. Similarly, in 1911, a horrific crash on the Lehigh Valley Railroad at Manchester, New York, killed 29 people and seriously injured another 60. This accident was attributed to that hidden menace: the transverse fissure. Like the causes of other major wrecks, rail fractures became a public issue. In an earlier era, such a disaster may have been shrugged off as unavoidable, but by this time action was required. In 1915, the Bureau of Standards initiated research to find a way to detect internal rail defects.

Dr. Elmer Sperry

One of the foremost inventors of the early twentieth century was Dr. Elmer Ambrose Sperry, a scientific genius who amassed more than 400 patents in his lifetime. He is probably best known for his gyroscopic inventions, including the gyrocompass. He also designed electrical equipment for streetcars and early electric locomotives, and worked on designs for electric automobiles. Between 1923 and 1928, Sperry developed an induction system that was capable of detecting internal rail defects, including transverse fissures, and he founded the Sperry Rail Service. It was immediately successful, and he built a fleet of Sperry Rail cars to inspect American railroads for hidden rail defects. Sperry initially hoped to sell the defect detection cars directly to the railroads, but he eventually concluded that it would be more practical to run a company that used the cars as a contract service for the railroads. While railroads today routinely contract many specialized services to outside vendors, in the late 1920s this was a relatively unusual practice. Railroads tended to be self-sufficient enterprises, keeping most of their maintenance work in house. Dr. Sperry died in 1930, but by the end of that year Sperry Rail Service had 10 large defect detection cars in operation, as well as a fleet of smaller rail defect detection equipment.

Sperry's Yellow Doodlebugs

Sperry Rail's large defect detection cars, known in the industry simply as Sperry cars, were built from self-propelled gasoline-electric cars and called "Doodlebugs." Doodlebugs were built for

verse fissure—an internal crack bisecting the width of the rail. This crack was especially dangerous because it was undetectable by traditional methods, yet it could cause the rail to break or even shatter under the weight of a train, causing a derailment.

In the years leading up to World War I, American railroads began to suffer the backlash of negative public sentiment, fueled by years of abuse of the public trust. Feuding rail barons, ambitious tycoons, rate wars, poor service, horrific crashes, and a general callousness toward passengers and shippers resulted in a tide of legislation aimed at curtailing railroad monopolies and man-

Built from self-propelled gas-electric cars known as "Doodlebugs," Sperry Rail Service's yellow inspection cars have been a common sight along America's railways for many years. Sperry No. 126, photographed at Fulshear, Texas, on July 17, 1997, retains some of its gas-electric character, including the old "cow catcher"– style pilot. *Tom Kline*

passenger service. The single gas-electric cars were cheaper to operate than a steam locomotive, and in the decade prior to World War I, gas-electric cars were a popular way for railroads to cut costs on branch-line passenger operations. The market for gas-electrics sagged during the war years, but enjoyed a healthy resurgence in the 1920s. Most American railroads bought Doodlebugs and assigned them to lightly patronized operations. A number of manufacturers built gas-electrics, including J. G. Brill, and the St. Louis Car Company. The Electro-Motive Corporation was one of the largest producers of gas-electric cars, although it didn't actually build the cars itself, but contracted the assembly to other builders. Electro-Motive was later bought by General Motors, and evolved into America's foremost diesel-electric locomotive manufacturer.

For the first large defect detection cars, Sperry bought new gas-electrics from J. G. Brill and

Dr. Elmer Sperry's induction testing revolutionized the way railroads search for hidden rail flaws. The black-and-yellow Sperry railcar has been an institution on American rails for more than 70 years.

outfitted them with detection equipment and living quarters for the crew. By the early 1930s, passenger business was in serious decline, and many railroads were discontinuing lightly patronized and unprofitable passenger services, resulting in a surplus of gas-electrics. As Sperry's business grew, it acquired many additional gas-electric cars secondhand from railroads. The gas-electric had largely vanished by the late 1960s, and later Sperry detection cars were home built by Sperry Rail. Over the years, Sperry amassed a roster of more than 25 self-propelled cars, many of which began their service lives as gas-electric passenger cars for various Class I railroads, including Seaboard Air Line, Baltimore & Ohio, Lehigh Valley, and Chicago & North Western.

Living on board the cars for weeks and months at a time, Sperry crews are treated to some of the finest scenery in the United States. Here SRS 118 descends California's Donner Pass, near Cape Horn, on April 26, 1991. This car was built for the Baltimore & Ohio in 1927.

which has been used in one variation or another for more than five decades. Sperry's self-propelled detection cars are numbered in the 100 series. Numbers 143 through 149, and car 200, are all home built; many of the earlier 100 series cars were constructed from gas-electrics or other railroad equipment.

Although Sperry is moving away from the larger detection cars, it still employs about 23 of them. The large cars are self-sufficient, and they are among the last examples of railroad equipment fitted with living spaces for the crew. (At one time the common caboose, among other pieces of equipment, was a home away from home for railroad employees, but the days of railroad crews living on their cabooses ended years ago.) The nature of the work brings Sperry cars all over the country, and gives their crews the opportunity to see many different places. Some cars are assigned to a specific region where they perform most of their testing; others travel far and wide. The crew often stays with the car for months at a time while it is on the road. After a full day of testing out on the line, the car ties up overnight on a siding or in a nearby railroad yard.

In addition to the testing and propulsion equipment, a Sperry detector car has a comfortable living space. Each car is designed to accommodate three or four Sperry employees. At the front of the car is the motor compartment, behind it is the galley where meals are prepared, and beyond that is the dining and lounge area. The middle of the car is equipped with upper and lower berths, a toilet, and shower facilities; a generator and storage space are found toward the rear of the car. The detection equipment, recording apparatus, and work area are located at the far end. An employee monitors the detection equipment checking for rail defects as the car rolls along the tracks.

The business of rail testing grew rapidly in Sperry's first few decades. In 1930, after less than two full years in business, Sperry Rail Service had tested 36,000 miles of track. Twenty years later, the company had tested more than 2,000,000 miles of track on 124 different railroads. Quite an accomplishment for such a small company.

Testing Methods

Every defect that Sperry finds prevents a potential wreck. No one can ever really know how

In the process of outfitting secondhand cars for defect-detection use, Sperry greatly altered their appearance, removing seats, blanking up windows, and adding the assorted equipment needed for rail testing. The traditional gasoline engines were gradually replaced with more modern diesel engines. The Sperry cars are typified by their striking yellow-and-black paint scheme,

Sperry No. 129, seen here on the Montana Rail Link at Helena, was built by the Electro-Motive Corporation and St. Louis Car Company for the Lehigh Valley Railroad in 1925. The ultrasonic detection equipment is visible between the wheels of the car. *Patrick Yough*

Union Pacific (UP) has a long tradition of maintaining its own inspection cars. UP's Plasser EC-3 track geometry car is seen at Houston, Texas, on February 20, 1988, when the car was brand-new. *Tom Kline*

The use of both systems allows the detection cars to locate a greater number of rail defects and with a greater degree of accuracy. Magnetic induction tests are most effective on the rail head, and may not reveal flaws in the body of the rail. In addition, some rail defects, such as fatigue cracks, may be disguised by other imperfections and are not revealed by induction testing. Bolt head cracks at the end of rails are among the defects that can be detected more reliably by the ultrasonic system. Sperry often uses ultrasonic inspection to complement its traditional testing, and both systems have proven useful for a thorough rail inspection. If a defect is found with one system, it can often be confirmed with the other, an especially important feature considering that many defects are invisible to the eye.

Induction Testing

Induction testing creates a powerful magnetic field in the rail, using large amounts of low-voltage current. Electrical brushes contact the rail to set up the magnetic field, while a sensing coil detects changes in the field that may indicate the existence of a rail flaw. Changes in the field are logged on a paper strip chart with automatic pens. Traditionally, one pen recorded changes in the field for each of the two rails. A highly skilled operator monitors the strip chart and interprets the incoming data. Magnetic induction can detect transverse fissures, but it also senses other imperfections in the rail, many of which are not serious. Corrosion, seams, and joints are all revealed by induction testing, so it is important to distinguish these from the more serious defects. When testing, Sperry cars roll along at just 6.5 to 13 miles per hour. When a potential defect has been located, the car stops and a crewman gets out to inspect the problem area and mark it for repair if necessary. Minor problems are indicated with yellow paint, more serious flaws with red paint. A railroad official typically rides along with the detection crew, and a repair gang shadows the car to make spot repairs.

Ultrasonic Testing

While the big Sperry cars still do induction testing, Sperry has gradually advanced its ultrasonic technology since it was first introduced more than 50 years ago, and major improvements in ultrasonic testing have made that system much more useful than it was in the early years. Sperry's first all ultrasonic railcar was built for the New York City Transit Authority for use on the city's subway system. This car was made from a Mack railbus built for the New Haven Railroad.

In ultrasonic testing, transducers project high-frequency sound impulses into the rails and rail

many derailments have been avoided, or how many lives have been saved by defect detection and preventative rail maintenance. The frequency with which different railroad routes are tested for defects varies greatly according to the level and type of traffic that is moved over the railroad, and with the needs of the owning railroad.

In their first two decades, Sperry cars employed a system using magnetic induction to test for defects. Then, beginning in the early 1950s, Sperry began augmenting the traditional induction tests with new ultrasonic tests. By the mid-1960s, all the big Sperry cars were equipped for both induction and ultrasonic testing.

For years Conrail operated its own track geometry train. The train consisted of two traditional passenger cars equipped with track geometry measuring and recording equipment. Conrail's No. 1933, a General Electric B23-7 locomotive, was semi-permanently assigned to the track geometry train. On a splendid October 7, 1997, the train rolls west on the old Boston & Albany mainline at Becket, Massachusetts. Conrail's track geometry train was a regular visitor to the B&A each autumn.

joints. The reflection of the sound is recorded, giving inspectors an image that reveals internal and external rail conditions. Manual ultrasonic tests were performed before it was practical to do ultrasonic testing from the Sperry car. A number of hurdles needed to be overcome before the cars could perform rolling ultrasonic tests. For example, early ultrasonic systems were easily affected by the presence of grease on the rail. The introduction of automated compensation systems solved this problem.

The typical transducer is coupled to the rail using a Roller Search Unit (RSU), which is basically a fluid-filled tire that rolls along below the

car. Inside the RSU are three transducer heads that project sound at three different angles. The different projection angles optimize the information that can be obtained from the inspection, similar to the visual effect of three cameras aimed at the same spot from different angles. The signal from the different heads is amplified, processed, and combined electronically to provide the most accurate rail profile; traditionally the ultrasonic system was monitored in the same basic fashion as the induction system, using ink pens and paper strip charts. Taking ultrasonic impulses from three different angles also minimizes detection errors caused when routine imperfections, such as normal bolt holes, are mistaken for actual flaws. Still, extra attention must be given to bolt holes, because these areas are especially subject to stress-related fractures. Different parts of the rail have different inspection requirements. The joint areas are particularly important, as they have unusually high stress and are prone to different types of flaws than the rest of the rail.

The advances in rail defect technology have helped railroads reduce the number of defects and repair problems before they lead to accidents. Though the railroads run far fewer trains than they once did, most mainlines carry significantly more tonnage than they did 50 years ago. Trains are longer and heavier than ever before, placing much greater stress on rails and track structure and making defect detection extremely important.

Left
Long Island Rail Road No. TC81 is a specially equipped Plasser-120 track geometry car designed for work on suburban electrified lines in the New York City metropolitan area. It is seen here at Metro-North's Maintenance of Way repair shop in North White Plains, New York on September 28, 2000. *Patrick Yough*

Plasser track geometry cars are versatile and adaptable, allowing them to be used by railways all around the world, including Iarnród Éireann (Irish Rail). Iarnród Éireann tracks are 5-foot, 3-inch gauge, but the loading gauge is restrictive by both American and continental European standards.

Measuring the gauge on the Southern Pacific at Siskiyou Summit, Oregon. The standard track width in North America, Britain, and most of Europe is 4 feet, 8.5 inches. While some minor variation in gauge can be tolerated, any significant deviation must be corrected.

Hyrail Detection Trucks

In addition to its large railcars, Sperry also has a fleet of Hyrail trucks (see Chapter 6). For many years, the trucks couldn't carry induction equipment and were limited to ultrasonic testing. Recently Sperry has developed a new induction system for use on its Hyrail trucks, and built a prototype truck capable of doing both types of testing. Eventually Sperry hopes to retire many of its older railcars, some of which are now more than 60 years old, and replace them with dual-inspection Hyrail trucks. Today's railroads prefer Hyrail vehicles because they are easier to get on and off the tracks. This gives a railroad greater flexibility when testing, as the truck can be taken off at almost any highway grade crossing, and doesn't need to tie up the tracks as severely as the big cars. This is an important consideration for modern railroads, which are trying to squeeze as much tonnage over as little track as

they can. The less time track is out of service for testing, the better.

Although the Hyrail detection vehicle will largely supplant the traditional "Doodlebug" detector car, Sperry will not replace all its big cars. There are still some situations where they are preferred, such as remote lines, where there are very few grade crossings and no local accommodation, as well as heavily traveled passenger routes, such as the Northeast Corridor. Lines in remote regions of Canada will probably remain the stomping grounds for traditional Sperry cars for years to come.

Sperry Rail Today

Today Sperry Rail Service is a division of Rockwood, one of the world's fastest growing materials engineering and inspection companies. Among Sperry's customers are several of the large North American railroads, including Cana-

S perry cars are among the last active examples of Doodlebugs in North America and they are sought by museums when they are retired. In the 1980s, Sperry donated car No. X107 to the Railroad Museum of New England, now located at Waterbury, Connecticut. There are plans to fix up the car and display it as a Brill Doodlebug. The preserved X107 has a unique history. Originally numbered 107, it was built new by J. G. Brill and assembled at New York Central's West Albany shops in 1930, and Sperry equipped the car with induction testing equipment. It was one of a few cars that fulfilled Dr. Sperry's original business plan, and unlike the majority of cars that were operated by Sperry as a service, No. 107 was outfitted as a test car and operated by the New York Central. (New York Central and Union Pacific adhered to a self-sufficiency principle and preferred to do their own defect testing. Union Pacific still maintains its own defect detection cars.) With New York Central, the defect car carried the number X8015. It was 73 feet, 4 inches long, and powered by a 300-horsepower engine. An auxiliary 28-horsepower gas engine powered a 200-amp generator for generating the magnetic field. For almost 40 years X8015 worked New York

Central rails, searching for defects and preventing accidents. In 1969, shortly after New York Central and the Pennsylvania Railroad merged to form Penn Central, Sperry reacquired the car, numbering it X107.

New York Central operated another gas-electric in non-revenue service as a clearance detection car. This car, No. X8016, was built in 1928 as a standard Brill Model 500 car. Unlike the X8015, it spent nearly three decades in passenger service before being transformed into a detection car by Central's Beach Grove (Indiana) Shops in 1955. Originally numbered M-10, it was powered by a pair of Brill 250-horsepower engines (thus the Model 500 designation) and had seats for 65 or 66 passengers. As a clearance detection car, most of its side windows were blocked up, and it was equipped with feelers on its sides and roof. It was used to measure minimum loading–gauge clearances.

Other Sperry cars have been candidates for preservation, including car 140, built in 1966 using the shell of a New York City Transit Authority R-33 subway car. In September 1976, this unusual Sperry car was sent to Australia, where it worked until it was retired in 1990. In May 2000, the car was moved to the Dorrigo Steam Railway & Museum in New South Wales.

Preserved Sperry Cars

Car No. 131, displaying an older variation of Sperry's yellow-and-black paint scheme, was built in 1925 for the Lehigh Valley, operating as its No. 27, and went to Sperry in 1941. The traditional pilot is still apparent, pictured here at Dolton, Illinois, in 1983. *John Eagan*

The CSX EM-GRMS track car is one of the most advanced detection cars on the railroad today. It is jointly manufactured by ENSCO and Plasser American. The body of the car is based on Plasser's PTS-62 track stabilizer car.

dian Pacific, CSX, Norfolk Southern, Burlington Northern Santa Fe, and Amtrak. Recently Sperry expanded its international market and started serving SJ, Sweden's national railway. Sperry Car No. 200, built new by Sperry in Danbury, Connecticut, was shipped to Sweden in May 1999. The car is manned by Sperry crews searching for defects on SJ. Sperry hopes to further expand its business in Europe and Asia and is looking at Eastern Europe as one of the best emerging new markets for its services.

Although Sperry Rail Service is the most prominent rail defect detection service, it is not the only one, and several other companies also offer a rail defect detection service; among the most prominent are Harsco and Herzog. Sperry is the only company that offers both induction and ultrasonic testing. A few railroads also perform their own testing instead of contracting the work to outside services.

Track Geometry Cars

The growth in the size and weight of trains has placed ever greater pressures on railroad infrastructure, while the mechanization of railroad maintenance has drastically reduced the number of employees needed to repair tracks. As a result, it is now more important than ever before to ensure that tracks and right-of-ways are maintained to proper standards. The operation of track geometry cars is an integral part of a modern railroad's maintenance program. These cars help

railroad managers make maintenance decisions based on detailed, accurate, and up-to-date information. The car's precise record of a line reveals potential future trouble spots as well as existing flaws. The cars are also used for judging maintenance quality when it is completed. Among the factors that a track geometry train measures are track gauge, profile (vertical change in the rail), and alignment (horizontal change in the rail). They also measure and record the degree of curvature, where a curve begins and ends, the amount of cross level (a measure of superelevation in curves), and the speed limitations imposed by a curve. In addition, they record the locations of crossings, switches, and other complicated track arrangements, providing a comprehensive database for future reference.

As with locating rail cracks and defects, track geometry measurement was traditionally within the realm of track walkers and local maintenance supervisors. By inspecting ties, spikes, and ballast conditions, the track walker looked for gauge imperfections and other abnormalities. Signs of unusual rail wear, loose spikes, and evidence of rail motion were signs that the tracks might not be holding up under load. Although his years of experience would often allow a track walker to identify areas in need of attention, even the best trained track walker couldn't identify everything that was wrong with the track, nor would he be able to accurately record every foot of mainline track for later analysis.

Many railroads regularly operate their own track geometry trains. A traditional geometry train was often a semi-permanently coupled two-car consist hauled by a locomotive. Old passenger cars were commonly converted into track geometry trains by outfitting them with specialized sensing and recording equipment. These trains would make routine scheduled trips over the line, recording the state of the tracks and right-of-way. For example Conrail's track geometry train consisted of two heavyweight passenger cars painted in dark "Pullman" green with yellow lettering that clearly identified it. It was almost always assigned the same locomotive, General Electric B23-7 No. 1933, as it made its yearly rounds across the system.

Over the years, the technology for track geometry measurements has made great progress. Today's track geometry cars use a variety of sophisticated technology to measure and record track conditions as they roll along. Laser technology, video cameras, and precision computerized measurement provide a level of detail that was not available in earlier eras. The coupling of video imaging with older measurement systems has resulted in a new breed of track geometry cars that permit high-speed analysis of track conditions. The Federal Railroad Administration's instrumentation contractor, ENSCO, has developed technology that is capable of operating at speeds up to 125 miles per hour for testing on Amtrak's Northeast Corridor. In addition to analyzing track conditions, ENSCO cars can provide a profile of the overhead electrified catenary (the network of wires used to provide electricity to power the trains).

Plasser EM-120

Plasser American produces a line of Engineering Inspection Vehicles, which not only measure track geometry but may fulfill other elements of railway maintenance as well. Among these is the EM-120, a self-propelled car 49 feet long, 10 feet wide, 13 feet tall, and weighing just 58.5 tons. These dimensions conform to the loading-gauge of most standard track gauge–railways in North America and around the world, making the car adaptable for operation on many different types of railways. Like other track geometry cars, the EM-120 measures and plots the distance between the rails and assesses rail wear, while calculating rail profile, alignment, superelevation, and gauge changes. As with other modern track geometry cars, the EM-120 uses a laser measurement system. Lasers project a light envelope on both sides of the running rails and measure the shadow to assess the level of wear. Computer analysis then determines the amount of wear by width and height,

the angle of the rail to the roadbed, and the amount of railhead extension beyond its normal cross section, sometimes described as the rail lip. Rail measurements typically are made every 6 feet as the car travels along at speeds of 40 to 60 miles per hour. Track geometry measurements are plotted on a graph for later analysis. In addition to the graphing, notable defects in track geometry are noted in special reports that indicate the location, length, and degree of seriousness of each perceived defect. To further aid in track assessment, the car is equipped with video cameras that make a detailed tape of the track. Location information, such as the railroad milepost, is superimposed on the video image to give track maintainers a solid frame of reference when looking at the tape.

The EM-120 can be equipped with a thermal imaging system designed for analysis of electrified third rails. Such specialized cars can be used by suburban railways and transit lines with third-rail electrification. For example the Long Island Rail Road operates a Plasser-120 No. TC81 on its suburban electrified lines in the New York City metropolitan area. The Long Island has the most extensive third-rail electrification in the United States, and one of the highest passenger ridership of any railroad in North America. The thermal imaging system employed by Long Island on its TC81 is based on the technology used for military night-vision goggles, which create a visual picture from temperature readings. The infrared scanner is mounted on the nose of the car, and is designed to allow both panning and tilting adjustment to give the best coverage of the tracks. The thermal images are recorded on videotape and routinely analyzed by a computer. Though a defect in the third rail is unlikely to cause a derailment, as would a typical rail defect, it can cause serious disruptions in service.

Every year, the Long Island's TC81 makes four complete inspections of the railroad's mainlines, and it checks major junctions and yard facilities twice a year. The car is designed to issue three categories of defect reports, according to the level of seriousness of the defect: The first are the parameters set for passenger comfort, the second is the railroad's own safety requirements, and the third is the Federal Railway Administration's requirements. The Long Island Rail Road is looking to improve its track geometry detection with a new car that will incorporate differential Global Positioning System (GPS) technology and the Gage Restraint Measurement System (GRMS).

Gauge Measurement

One of the most modern varieties of railroad detection cars uses the Gage Restraint Measurement System (GRMS) to evaluate track conditions,

The EM-GRMS uses the Gage Restraint Measurement System, which has a hydraulically powered adjustable split-axle device to apply large amounts of lateral pressure on the rails. The GRMS simulates the effects of a passing train in order to evaluate track gauge under load.

plan the replacement of ties, and judge the effectiveness of track maintenance programs. The standard track gauge on American tracks is 4 feet, 8.5 inches, and wheel flanges on normal railway wheels allow for some variation in gauge without risk of derailment. Still, track that is out of gauge is one of the top-five culprits of modern railroad derailments. A report by Gary A. Carr and Cameron Stuart indicates that 1,838 accidents involving gauge widening were reported by the Federal Railroad Administration between 1984 and 1990. The vast majority of these were the result of missing or defective ties or rail fasteners. A passing train places tremendous vertical and lateral forces on track, which can cause the rails to spread enough to cause the wheel to drop between them. This situation is most acute in curves, where centrifugal force puts added stress on the outside rail.

As with the detection of other track flaws, the traditional methods of looking for gauge deficiencies eventually became ineffective for modern railroads. Simply measuring the distance between the rails using conventional track gauging devices does not reveal fundamental structural flaws in the track that can result in a gauge-widening derailment. While track inspectors may take careful note of the condition of ties, tie plates, and fasteners, there is still an untold story. Gauge widening can be caused by a combination of conditions,

including cracked and deteriorated ties, broken tie plates, and loose spikes. It is not always cost-effective, however, to constantly repair every visual flaw in track, so guidelines have been drawn up that aid in assessing track conditions. A single rotten tie is not going to cause a gauge-widening incident, but at some stage, enough rotten ties in a given section of track can lead to problems. The speed and weight of trains and the level of traffic on a section of track are significant considerations in determining whether repairs are warranted. Each class of track has a certain level of flaws that are permissible. The evaluation of track is largely subjective, and each inspector has to use his own judgment in determining track conditions. Furthermore, some flaws are invisible to visual detection and go unnoticed. A vital consideration in effective gauge evaluation is that a heavy train presents a very different set of track conditions than exist on track without a train on it. Thus evaluating empty track provides a skewed analysis from the get-go. The development of GRMS is a vast improvement over conventional methods because it simulates the forces of a heavy train on track during the evaluation to provide a more accurate assessment.

The GRMS uses a special hydraulically powered adjustable split-axle device to put pressure on the track while special sensors monitor responses in the track. The split axle places 14,000 pounds of lateral force and 19,000 pounds of vertical force on the tracks in order to make measurements. This may seem like a fairly strong pressure, but the amount of lateral and vertical force is somewhat less than would be applied by an actual train. To compensate for the differences, an onboard computer extrapolates the data to paint a more accurate picture of how a train stresses the tracks.

The GRMS is used by a special track geometry car, designated EM-GRMS, that is manufactured jointly by ENSCO and Plasser American. The body of the car is based on Plasser's PTS-62 track stabilizer car. It is 60 feet, 7 inches long; 9 feet, 3 inches wide; and 14 feet, 9 inches tall; and it weighs 80 tons. In addition to its GRMS functions, the car measures rail alignment, cross level, and the longitudinal profile of the rails. The EM-GRMS is powered by a 440-horsepower engine and is designed to take track geometry readings at speeds up to 50 miles per hour; when using GRMS, the car is limited to 35 miles per hour, remarkably fast considering the type of work it is performing.

The EM-GRMS outputs information for operators and track managers to study, while also marking serious track defects on-site using white and yellow paint. Areas marked with only white paint are less serious and are intended to flag the defect for further inspection within 30 days. Places marked with yellow paint or both white and yellow paint indicate serious gauging problems that need immediate corrective action. As stated earlier, the standard American track gauge is 4 feet, 8.5 inches. The white paint marks indicate that the gauge of the track under load is up to 4 feet, 10 inches, while the yellow paint designates loaded track gauge that exceeds 4 feet, 11 inches, or 2.5 inches wider than normal. Track this wide presents a high risk of derailment. Routine information obtained from the EM-GRMS can be used by railroad maintenance crews during scheduled track maintenance and can help identify ties that need replacing and related work.

Federal Railroad Administration

In the United States, the Federal Railroad Administration (known universally in the industry by its alphabet soup–style three-letter abbreviation, FRA) is responsible for setting and enforcing railroad safety standards. Since 1966 the FRA has performed automated safety inspections of American railroads. These inspections are important for monitoring compliance with Federal Track Safety Standards and helping the railroads to identify problem areas and plan maintenance programs.

Track safety inspectors use the FRA's Automated Track Inspection Program (ATIP) to identify potential track problems on key routes. Every year the FRA's ATIP inspects 25,000 to 30,000 miles of the American railway infrastructure, including lines served by Amtrak, routes deemed of strategic military importance, and routes used to transport hazardous materials, such as depleted nuclear fuels.

The FRA classifies track using strict standards to set maximum speeds for freight and passenger trains. The faster the class of track, the tighter the FRA standards. The lowest grade of track is Class 1, which allows a maximum speed of 10 miles per hour for freight and 15 for passenger trains. By contrast, Class 4 track permits a maximum speed of 60 miles per hour for freight and 80 miles per hour for passengers. In addition to meeting track geometry parameters, the faster classes of track also have to adhere to other safety requirements, such as signaling to protect against collisions.

In 1981, the FRA began using a special track geometry car designated T-10 for its Automated Track Inspection Program. This car was based on a Budd-built, diesel-powered SPV-2000 railcar—essentially a modern-day equivalent of the old gas-electric car—which used the same type of curved stainless-steel body introduced on the original Metroliners in the late 1960s and employed on Amtrak's Amfleet passenger cars. FRA's T-10 was 85.3 feet long, 10.5 feet wide, 14.5 feet high, and weighed 70 tons. It was capable of traveling at a maximum speed of 80 miles per hour. The T-10 could measure eight different aspects of track geometry, plotting them on magnetic tape and an oscillograph. Like other modern track geometry cars, the T-10 used sensors to take measurements that were fed to onboard computers for analysis. It measured the profile and alignment of each rail, and the gauge between them, while calculating the cross level, curvature, and warp of the track and comparing this information with the FRA's track safety standards.

To keep pace with changes in the industry and take advantage of new technologies, the FRA issued new safety standards in 1998. Among the changes were new requirements mandating more frequent rail inspections. An FRA press release dated June 25, 1998 explained:

> The new track standards permit each railroad to design its own electronic record-keeping system, as long as the system properly safeguards the integrity and authenticity of each record. Electronic record-keeping, which currently is allowed only through a lengthy waiver process, will aid railroads, as well as the FRA, in retrieving necessary information to assess the effectiveness of track maintenance programs.
>
> Under the old regulations, internal rail inspections were required once annually, with no consideration for

highly utilized trackage. Under the revised regulations, the frequency of internal rail inspections will be determined by a combination of elapsed time and the tonnage accumulated over the track since the last inspection. In addition, the requirement will now apply to all Class 3 trackage, which is capable of sustaining freight trains safely at 26 to 40 miles per hour and passenger trains at 31 to 60 miles per hour. Under the old regulations, the internal rail inspection requirements applied only to Class 3 trackage over which regularly scheduled passenger trains were operated.

In 1999, the FRA awarded a $3.7 million contract to ENSCO to produce a new state-of-the-art track car to replace the obsolete T-10. The new FRA vehicle was intended to take advantage of the latest developments, such as differential global positioning. At the time of the award, Federal Railroad Administrator Jolene M. Molitoris explained the benefits of the new car in a press release:

> The new track geometry measurement vehicle will advance safety, which is President Clinton's highest transportation priority. [The new vehicle] will enhance our track safety oversight capabilities and thus help assure safe movement, especially of passengers and hazardous materials.

Ultimately two new vehicles were constructed: a new self-propelled car, designated T-2000, to replace the T-10; and a research platform, designated T-16, for developing new track inspection technology. The T-2000 can travel up to 90 miles per hour under its own power, but it can perform tests at speeds up to 110 miles per hour when towed along in a train. The T-16 can work at speeds as fast as 150 miles per hour. The new cars were unveiled at Washington Union Station in November 2000, just a few weeks before the debut of America's fastest passenger train, the *Acela Express* (which can travel at a top speed of 150 miles per hour in revenue service, a significant increase over previous top speeds).

The Federal Railroad Administration's T-10 detection car rolls past the Scoular grain elevator at Silver Bow, Montana, on September 6, 2000. After two decades testing American railroads, the uniquely designed car is being replaced by more sophisticated equipment.
Patrick Yough

3

Ballast and Roadbed Maintenance

Good drainage is essential to a solid track structure, and drainage is accomplished with proper ballasting and trackside ditches. High quality ballast is the key to good track structure and overall stability. Failure to properly maintain ballast will result in a gradual deterioration of the roadbed and subsequently the degradation of the tracks. If minor drainage problems and clogged ballast are left unchecked, they can lead to a serious maintenance problem and result in lower safe speeds and increase the likelihood of derailments.

One measure of a railroad company's financial health is the condition of its tracks. A railroad with well-maintained, high-quality ballast shows that the company has allocated its resources toward proper maintenance and has a long-term outlook. By contrast, a railroad with poor ballast, low rail joints, and uneven track has neglected the very foundation of its track structure, and has cut corners for short-term gain. Excessively dirty, weedy, and unkempt ballast indicate more serious problems, both with the track structure and with the railroad company itself. When a railroad is tight for cash and looking to trim expenditures, cutting funds for

Illinois Central's Memphis to Grenada local carefully treads through high water at Blanche, Mississippi, in April 1994. Proper ditching and ballast maintenance is designed to draw water away from the track structure. Flooding that brings water up to the level of the rail is extremely damaging to the tracks. *Mike Abalos*

track maintenance, particularly such projects as ballast renewal, is an easy way to save money in the short term. But ignoring fundamental maintenance is a gamble. In effect the company is mortgaging its future—and at a very high interest rate.

Dirt Below the Surface

Fresh ballast is designed to drain water away from the center of the tracks into ditches along the right-of-way. The ditches then carry the water away from the roadbed. Most modern railroads use crushed rock for ballast on the mainline. It is the most expensive conventional kind of ballast, but it has also proven to be the most effective. Crushed rock does a good job of holding the track in place, and it provides excellent drainage.

A Montana Rail Link track worker manually dumps ballast along the tracks at Muir, Montana, on September 21, 1994. Ballast cars are specially designed to direct ballast on the tracks with chutes that can send the stone to either side of the rail. In this case ballast is directed outside the rail. *Tom Kline*

Crushed stone flexes beneath the weight of a passing train while remaining firm to hold the ties in place. Crushed stone is less prone to disintegration and cementing than other forms of ballast, yet all ballast gradually becomes fouled. Even stone ballast eventually breaks down and crumbles, becoming abraded as a result of passing railway traffic and the cyclical freezing and thawing imposed by nature. Fine particles of abraded ballast, combined with natural dust and dirt, and debris that has fallen from passing trains, conspire to clog ballast, limiting its ability to drain water properly. In addition, fouling matter in the sub-ballast and sub-grade tend to work up through the good ballast, mix with water, and turn into mud. The mud then effectively seals off the crib between the ties and acts as a dam, preventing proper drainage and damaging the track.

Understanding how ballast clogs makes it easier to establish corrective measures to solve the problem and restore tracks to good condition. Ballast clogging is a vicious circle. As the ballast becomes clogged, its ability to drain properly deteriorates, and water gets trapped in the ballast, causing further damage that compounds the situation. When the ballast becomes waterlogged, the up-and-down action of the wheels of a train passing on the track pumps water and debris from the sub-ballast, drawing it to the surface and further soiling the ballast. When severe pumping occurs, mud and water can be clearly seen around the ties and joints. This pumping is aggravated in track sections with poor rail joints, where there is greater movement caused by excessive pounding. As a result, tracks with traditional jointed rail are more prone to

The Boston & Maine NW2 No. 1206 powers a traditional shoulder ballast cleaner. The mechanized ballast cleaner is not a new concept; these machines have been around for many years. *H. Bentley Crouch*

this type of ballast deterioration than modern welded rail, in which the joints are normally separated by as much as 1,500 feet, instead of each rail having a joint every 39 feet. The problem of clogged and cemented ballast is also more prone to occur on steeply graded lines, where locomotives are constantly laying down sand on the rails to gain traction. Heavily used railroads, such as heavy coal and ore lines that carry a huge amount of material that can fall on the tracks, suffer from more rapid ballast degradation than lines with cleaner traffic.

The depth of ballast and sub-ballast below it varies greatly from railroad to railroad, depending on the type of traffic hauled, the age of the route, and the type of ballast used. Traditional mainlines, particularly those in the eastern and midwestern United States, tend to have the deepest layer of ballast and sub-ballast, as a result of years of ballast renewal. One conventional method of track renewal was to dump fresh ballast across the tracks, and then jack the track—ties, rails, and all—through the layer of ballast and tamp it down. In this scenario, the old ballast often becomes sub-ballast. On some older lines, the combined layer of ballast and sub-ballast runs more than 3 feet deep below the ties. Normally tracks should not be lifted more

than about 8 inches during ballast renewal; if the tracks are lifted higher than that, there is high risk of uneven settling, a condition that may prove more troublesome than clogged ballast.

Ballast Cleaners and Undercutters

Repeatedly dumping ballast on tracks has its limitations. Every time ballast is added to the tracks, the tracks get a few inches higher. This begins to present problems at underpasses and other places with limited overhead clearance. Ballast cleaning has long provided a solution for difficulties with fouled ballast. In the days before mechanized track machinery, ballast cleaning, like nearly all railroad maintenance, was accomplished by hand. Men with picks and shovels removed soiled ballast and ran it through a sieve to shake out foreign matter. The ballast was then replaced manually. It has been a long time since American railroads relied on this primitive method of ballast cleansing. Since the steam era, machines have been designed to do this job faster and more effectively than it could be done by hand. Shoulder ballast cleaners are one such tool. These machines are designed to clean the ballast along the edge of the tracks. Though this method cleans only 30 to 40 percent of the ballast on the

Conrail's C30-7A No. 6596 leads a Speno shoulder cleaner at Auburndale, Massachusetts, on July 18, 1985, clearing the debris at the end of the ties. Such debris causes damming in the cribbing between the ties. The shoulder cleaner removes the dams to restore proper drainage, allowing the ballast to function as it is intended. *H. Bentley Crouch*

right-of-way and leaves the majority of the ballast between the ties untouched, the theory behind it is that if the shoulder is cleaned and profiled properly, the muddy dams will be broken, allowing the natural drainage of the track to flush unwanted debris and silt from the cribbing area between the ties.

A shoulder cleaning ballast machine rolls along on the tracks at a working speed of just 1 to 2 miles per hour. It excavates ballast on both sides of the track as close to the tie ends as it can without the risk of damaging them. The dirty ballast is deposited on a set of large vibrating screens within the machine. The screens serve the same function as the old sieves, separating out the ballast from unwanted debris. The cleaned ballast is re-

deposited along the track, while the debris is sent by rotary conveyor into hoppers that are hauled along by the train, or it is thrown a safe distance from the tracks. Since dumping the debris back onto the right-of-way is not always feasible, a ballast cleaning train might tow several hoppers along behind it. The amount of work a ballast cleaner can do is limited by the capacity of its hopper train. When the hoppers are filled, the train must travel to a designated landfill to dump the debris before it can continue its ballast cleaning. The rate at which the hoppers are filled depends on the rate of ballast cleaning and how soiled the ballast has become.

A modern shoulder ballast cleaner manufactured by Loram excavates between 2 and 2.5 feet

This shoulder cleaner uses its large cutting wheels to remove ballast along the side of the track. The material is then sifted to remove sand, dirt, and foreign matter that causes fouling, and the ballast is dumped back on the tracks, while the fouling matter is thrown to the side or dumped into hopper cars towed along with the cleaner. *John Eagan*

it is completely fouled cannot be effectively corrected by shoulder cleaning. In these cases it may be necessary to remove the ballast with undercutting machinery and then completely replace it. Undercutting is also used where insufficient vertical clearance prohibits the raising of tracks during ballast renewal, such as on lines that pass through long tunnels or through urban areas with numerous overhead bridges. In these instances, undercutting may be the only effective way to restore proper drainage.

Some undercutting machines use a continuous chain placed below the tracks to scoop away ballast and debris. Others use a large rotary wheel to dig a lineside trench and a bar placed below the tracks to remove fouled ballast. As with ballast cleaners, an undercutter can deposit the material into hoppers with a conveyer or distribute it well away from the tracks to keep the old ballast from interfering with drainage. Since an undercutter does not return any material to the roadbed, it tends to fill hoppers more quickly than ballast cleaners. While a ballast cleaner just deposits fouling material in the hoppers, an undercutter deposits everything it scoops up. Modern ballast machines sometimes combine undercutting and ballast cleaning functions.

Harsco Track Technologies' Trac-Gopher (Model GO-4S) is a 100,000-pound undercutter designed for mainline and switch/highway-crossing work. Using a 12-foot, 7-inch trenching wheel, it is designed to cut a 20-inch-wide trench up to 34 inches deep alongside the track. The trenching wheel can be laterally adjusted, allowing the trench to be located anywhere from immediately adjacent to the ties to up to 9 feet from the center of the track. Once a preliminary trench is excavated, a 15-foot-long, 6-inch-deep cutting bar is placed below the tracks to remove ballast from below the ties. The bar is adjustable to allow undercutting from 6.5 inches to 2 feet, 3 inches deep. The undercutter is powered by an eight-cylinder General Motors diesel engine that runs at 1,200 rpm, generating 364 horsepower. The undercutter runs on four 30-inch wheels and has 15,000 pounds tractive effort, enough to tow up to four 100-ton loaded ballast cars on level tangent track.. Undercutting spoil is transferred to a conveyor that can throw it as much as 45 feet from the track, or deposit it in ballast cars. While the Trac-Gopher has a travel speed of

of ballast beyond the tie ends on either side of the track, and reaches down 6 inches below the tie level. It also employs a scarifier to the tie ends to remove the silt and mud that has dammed the crib area and impeded drainage. Loram machines have built-in ballast regulators and brooms that contour and trim the ballast to the correct profile after it has been cleaned and redeposited along the sides of the track.

While shoulder ballast cleaning can be the most cost-effective way to restore proper drainage to a line suffering from clogged and contaminated ballast, it has its limitations. Ballast can only be cleaned so many times before it breaks down to the point where it is no longer effective. In addition, ballast that has deteriorated to the point that

Conrail's Dirt Devil undercutter churns away at Milepost 81 along the Boston & Albany. In the 1980s, many lines used specialized machines such as this one to increase their mainline clearances in order to accommodate taller trains.

up to 25 miles per hour when it isn't undercutting, its working speed is just 2 to 10 feet per minute. At this speed, it can undercut a maximum of 600 feet of track per hour. The machine itself is 15 feet tall; 10 feet, 6 inches wide; and 40 feet long. Unlike traditional undercutters that had minimalist wire-frame cabs, the Trac-Gopher has a comfortable, completely enclosed operator's cab. It is relatively spacious inside, and is insulated, pressurized, and equipped with a heater and an optional air conditioner.

In addition to ballast renewal considerations, railroads may decide to undercut track as a way to increase clearances. In situations where it is physically difficult, prohibitively expensive, or politically impossible to raise vertical clearances, undercutting is an attractive alternative for improving clearances on the line. In the mid-1960s, the Pennsylvania Railroad chose to undercut portions of its Philadelphia-Harrisburg mainline to better accommodate tri-level autoracks. The line is electrified with overhead catenary, energized with 11,000-volt alternating current. Prior to its

The undercutter uses an excavating chain placed below the tracks to remove ballast and soil from beneath the ties. As the machine moves forward (to the left in the photo), the debris is dropped in a hopper (seen on the right), which sends it away from the tracks via conveyor belt.

clearance improvement project, Pennsylvania Railroad experienced occasional difficulties with wires coming into contact with the tops of new automobiles on auto-carrying freight cars. (This was in the days before protected covered autoracks, and the cars simply ran out in the open.) One can just imagine the spark show when brand-new Chevys or Fords hit the wires! Undercutting was required where low overhead bridges forced the level of the wires too close to the tops of the cars.

In the mid-1980s, American railroads began to take advantage of deregulation, spurring the increased operation of double-stack container trains. At the same time, concerns from automobile manufacturers about vandalism to new cars riding in open autoracks led to the development of tri-level covered autoracks. Since these new types of railroad cars were several feet taller than most conventional cars, many railroads undertook massive clearance improvement programs to accommodate them. Again, undercutting was often the preferred option.

Ballast Trains

Fresh ballast is often needed during track work to replace soiled ballast or to replenish existing ballast, or it is laid down in preparation for new or relocated track. Ballast is typically quarried on line and distributed around the railroad in specially assigned ballast trains. While railroads may designate old coal hoppers or ore jennies for the task of transporting ballast, often they utilize more specialized equipment. Air-actuated side-dump cars are used to distribute large quantities of ballast to the sides of the right-of-way. The Difco dump car is a common type of commercially produced air-actuated dump car. For general distribution, specialized ballast hoppers are employed to haul and dump the stone. Since ballast is extremely heavy, ballast hoppers tend to be lower, shorter, and more durable than hoppers used for coal. Ballast hoppers are also designed to distribute their load along the tracks, and simple coal chutes are not the most effective way of doing this. A good ballast hopper can easily control the amount and direction of ballast dumped, and

Before the undercutter can get its cutting chain below track level, a backhoe removes ballast, and the tracks are jacked up. Here at Milepost 81 on the Boston & Albany route, the tracks are being lowered about 1 foot to increase the vertical clearance and permit the operation of tri-level covered autoracks and other tall cars.

The operator amenities in Conrail's Dirt Devil undercutter are minimal, but the controls are relatively straightforward.

directing the flow of ballast to either inside or outside the rails is an important function of the ballast trains. Traditionally, ballast was spread along the tracks very slowly, usually no faster than walking speed. As the ballast train crawled along, employees walked beside the train and distributed the ballast by opening and closing chutes as needed to regulate the flow.

Technology is catching up with conventional methods. In 2000, the Herzog Contracting Corporation, one of the leading lessors of ballast equipment, introduced a modern high-tech ballast delivery system known as the Programmed Linear Unloading System, or PLUS train. Where conventional ballast trains delivered ballast at less than 5 miles per hour, Herzog's PLUS train can dump ballast with precision accuracy at speeds up to 20 miles per hour. This space-aged ballast train uses modern computer and Global Positioning System technology to do its job. A skilled Herzog technician rides ahead of the PLUS train with a railroad representative, ideally a road foreman or track maintenance supervisor, and takes detailed notes as to the desired location and quantity of ballast needed. This information, along with the location of bridges, switches and obstructions that may interfere with ballast distribution, is logged on-site into a laptop computer. It is later downloaded to a computer on board the train, which uses the information when applying ballast. The hopper door controls are extremely sensitive, and designed to carefully regulate the flow of ballast to the track. The computer on board the train takes the speed of the train into account when delivering the ballast, adjusting the door openings to compensate for the speed. If the train is moving

faster, ballast needs to be dumped at a greater rate than if the train is moving slowly. This system minimizes problems caused when a ballast train slows abruptly during ballast spreading. The ballast doors on the PLUS train are larger, and open and close up to five times faster than on more conventional equipment, which permits the train to dump its load much more quickly. A PLUS train of 50 100-ton hoppers can deploy its entire load in less than an hour. Such a time saving is a great advantage to modern railroads with limited time windows available for track work. Since the entire train is automated and the ballast sites have been predetermined, it is unnecessary for railroad personnel to be on the ground, offering an additional saving for the railroad. Like other modern track-monitoring equipment, the PLUS train's survey system records the information and holds it for future ballasting needs. This allows a railroad to determine if a particular stretch of track is using an excessive amount of ballast over time, and appropriate remedial action can be taken. Herzog hopes that its new train will win favor with American railroads by its increased productivity and cost savings.

Ditch Diggers

Directing water away from the track is a routine yet extremely vital aspect of a railroad's maintenance program. Standing water undermines track stability, and as a result, drainage ditches are a standard part of railroad construction.

Traditional ditching methods were time-consuming, labor-intensive, and expensive. The work required large gangs of men along with steam shovels and other equipment. As railroad technology progressed, ditching moved from conventional manual methods to mechanization. One of the first mechanized ditching tools was the Jordan Spreader, discussed in detail later in the chapter. Though the Jordan was an excellent tool in its day, and some lines still use them, new more advanced machines have superseded the Jordan Spreader as the ditching tool of choice. Because today's railroads demand maximum track utilization, making maintenance windows precious commodities, specialized ditching machines have been developed that operate much faster, more cheaply, and more accurately than more conventional machines.

The primary objective of a ditch digger is to move away earth and water while profiling the land to create a drainage ditch. The ditch is designed to lower the water table around the tracks by drawing water away from the roadbed. To make the best use of a modern ditch digger, facilitate fast ditch digging, and minimize its time on the mainline, railroads will prepare a site in advance and clear away

Some railroads paint ballast fleets distinctively to distinguish them from revenue service cars. Union Pacific's ballast cars are treated with a forest green livery, Amtrak's are a brilliant safety orange, and Conrail's were a light gray that almost matched the color of the stone they carried. While many railroads assigned any surplus motive power to ballast service, a few have designated locomotive fleets for work or ballast trains.

Conrail obtained much of its ballast from a quarry in West Springfield, Massachusetts, along the old Boston & Albany route. Ballast quarrying is strictly seasonal business in New England because of the cold and sometimes snowy winters, so most of Conrail's ballast was delivered in the spring, summer, and early autumn. In season, a train or two of ballast would be loaded every day, and then hauled over Washington Mountain for distribution on the rest of Conrail's system. This was an especially difficult pull, involving a winding 1.67 percent climb between Chester and Washington. Conrail locomotives would slow to a crawl trying to haul the ballast trains over the hill. While most trains made it without serious problems, all too often a heavy ballast train would stall a few miles west of Chester, Massachusetts, as it entered the reverse curves at Milepost 129.

Conrail Ballast Express

For many years, Conrail's ballast trains warranted the same types of six-axle locomotives used by the other Conrail trains on the B&A. Toward the end of Conrail operations, before the railroad was divided by Norfolk Southern and CSX, Conrail reassigned its fleet of 10 General Electric C32-8s to Boston Line ballast service. These unique locomotives were delivered to Conrail in 1984 and spent much of their careers working on the Boston Line. The locomotives were unusual for several reasons: They were the only C32-8s ever built and they used a 12-cylinder FDL engine, instead of the far more common 16-cylinder FDL engine. Externally they had the Classic Dash 8 car body, with curving contoured cabs—a body style that was in production for only a few years. In the mid-1990s these locomotives were repainted from Conrail blue to a distinctive gray scheme and lettered for Ballast Express service. For several years they were regularly assigned to ballast work and hauled loaded stone trains all over the system. When there wasn't ballast work for them, Conrail used them on other Boston Line services. CSX also assigned some locomotives in work train service, painting them a bright safety orange and assigning them to ballast trains and other maintenance-of-way duties.

A pair of Conrail's unique General Electric C32-8s, in Ballast Express paint, work on the former Pennsylvania Railroad at Latrobe, Pennsylvania. The 10 Conrail C32-8s were the only examples of this type of locomotive. Conrail reassigned the fleet to work train service in the late 1990s. *Patrick Yough*

This Conrail ballast hopper has remote-controlled ballast doors that permit rapid spreading of ballast along the right-of-way. The car can carry up to 200,000 pounds of stone. Notice how the chutes are aimed to direct ballast to either side of the rail. *Patrick Yough*

This work train on the Cartier Railway in northern Quebec offers a good view of a dump car used to distribute ballast. It can dump to either side of the track. Because of its isolated nature, the Cartier still does most of its maintenance with traditional rail-based equipment.

A trackman on the Montana Rail Link adjusts the traps on loaded ballast cars in preparation for spreading the stone on the tracks.
Patrick Yough

debris. Anything that might damage, clog, or delay ditch digging machines is removed by workers and machines on the ground. This includes, for example, old crossties, fragments of broken rail, large rocks, and brush.

Loram, the maintenance equipment contractor known for its undercutting and rail grinding services (see chapter 5), also offers one of the most modern mechanized ditching machines. This able machine is named after the badger, a mammal known for its rapid burrowing ability. A badger can dig a hole with its paws much faster than a man could with his hands; likewise, Loram's Badger ditch digger is designed for greater speed and efficiency in digging trackside ditches. The Badger is a self-propelled machine that can attain a travel speed of 45 miles per hour, which gets it over the railroad fast when moving between work sites. It features two adjustable arms for digging. One carries a high-speed digging wheel to sculpt the ditch, and the other is a conveyor to remove earth and water from the digging site. The Badger can dig a ditch between 6 and 18 feet from the track center, and can cut down to 4 feet below the rail level. It can profile a ditch to most specifications required to improve track drainage. Many ditches can be dug with a single pass of the Bad-

ger, but some may require multiple passes, especially more complicated terraced ditches. The Badger works much faster than older machines, meaning more works gets done in less time. At its best, the Badger can move as much as 1,000 tons or 500 cubic yards of earth and water every hour. The conveyor can be aimed to deposit ditch waste up to 35 feet from the tracks, or into air-actuated side-dump cars carried along with the digging machine. The method of waste disposal depends on the area being ditched. Drainage problems often occur in deep rock cuts, and in such constraining environments, it is more convenient to use the dump cars for waste removal.

Unlike other elements of track geometry and roadbed design, ditch digging is a fairly inexact process. The theory behind ditch placement doesn't always work the way the railroad hopes it will. A ditch may function adequately under normal circumstances, draining runoff away from the roadbed and keeping the right-of-way sufficiently dry, but be inadequate for more extreme conditions. For example, railroad ditches have to accommodate a lot more water during heavy rains than they do on normal days. If they fail, tracks can flood or wash out. Washouts are relatively rare these days, and accidents caused by washouts

Canadian Pacific's D10 Ten-Wheeler No. 806 is assigned to work with a Jordan Spreader. This photo was made at Debec Junction, New Brunswick, on October 3, 1956. *H. Bentley Crouch*

Previous page

On July 12, 1978, a Canadian National Jordan Spreader shapes ballast as it is shoved along. The Jordan's adjustable wing was designed for this type of contouring work. Versatility was one of the Jordan's great attributes; this one machine could be fitted with more than a dozen different attachments. *H. Bentley Crouch*

even rarer. They can still happen, however, so maintenance crews must be on their toes, keeping drainage systems up to par and ready for the big 10-year or 50-year flood. In assessing ditch capacity, routine drainage and extreme flooding need to be considered separately.

When planning ditches along its lines, a railroad needs to weigh the costs of ditching against the risk and impact of severe floods. In some cases, no amount of trackside ditching will help, and in these situations other alternatives must be considered. For example, railroad lines that cross the Sacramento River Delta and flood plain are built on trestles, rather than embankments, even though most of the time the area below the tracks is bone-dry. When the flood does come, the trestle is the only way to go.

Jordan Spreaders

It is difficult to find a piece of equipment that is as universal and as useful for railroad maintenance as the Jordan Spreader. It is one of the oldest types of maintenance machines employed by modern railroads, and at one time it was among the most common. While it has largely been supplanted by more modern, specialized maintenance equipment, the traditional Jordan Spreader can still be found on many railroad lines. The Jordan can work as a ditching machine, a ballast regulator, and a heavy snowplow. It combines all these tools in one rugged, adaptable, low-tech piece of equipment. The Jordan is one of the last relics of the steam era still found on American railroads.

The Jordan Spreader is named for its inventor, Oswald F. Jordan, a one-time roadmaster for New York Central's Canada Southern Lines. In 1905, he left the railroad, and applied his years of experience to developing, building, and marketing a track maintenance tool that was superior to anything else available at the time. In the first few years, Jordan contracted the job of building his distinctive machines to various railroad shops. It wasn't until about 1911 that Jordan opened a factory and began manufacturing the spreaders himself. Jordan's factory was located in East Chicago, and it was always a relatively modest facility. For more than five decades the company built spreaders and snowplows, until the company was acquired by Jackson Vibrators in 1964. More than 1,100 Jordans were sold to railroads all around the country and Canada. Jackson-Jordan was one of the predecessors of today's Harsco Track Technologies.

The Jordan Spreader is a simple machine with relatively few moving parts and virtually no complicated machinery. As a result, it doesn't require much maintenance; it can be largely ignored for months at a time, and yet be ready to go at a moment's notice. It shares many qualities with older snowplow designs (discussed in greater detail in chapter 7). The basic Jordan has a pivoting front-mounted plow that can be angled to direct the material it is pushing to either side of the tracks. Each side of the machine is equipped with large adjustable wings that can be extended and locked into place. The wings are hinged near the front of the machine, and they are adjusted by large cylinders. Most Jordans built before the 1950s used air-actuated pneumatic cylinders; later machines were hydraulic, and they carried a small diesel engine on board to operate the hydraulic pump. A variety of different attachments could be applied to the Jordan's plow and wings, which was one reason for its popularity and versatility. Customized plow blades could be used to match the needs of the railroad. Many Jordan Spreaders came equipped with large snow-service plows and were intended as snowplows.

The Jordan, once used commonly as a ditching machine, is rarely used for ditching today. Many railroads had distinctive ditch-cutting blades that were designed to create a specific profile. Since the spreader has no power of its own, a locomotive has to shove it from behind in order for the spreader to do its work. The Jordan must be stationary when it is set up for ditching, and once it is ready, a locomotive will shove it along at about 5 miles per hour. The machine's operator can make minor adjustments, raising and lowering the wings with the cylinders, as required by the railroad's grading profile. Watching for signs along the right-of-way and taking cues from his experience, the Jordan operator keeps his eyes on the wings, while remaining in

Conrail's Jordans were painted bright safety yellow and equipped with large snow-service plows. This Jordan is seen along the former Erie Railroad Buffalo Line at Attica, New York, on May 8, 1988.

close communication with the locomotive engineer pushing him forward. In the days prior to radios on trains, this was a tricky business, and the Jordan operator, like most trainmen of the period, had to be well versed in nonverbal communication. Basic tasks can be accomplished with just a single well-planned pass of the Jordan, but more complicated ditching routinely requires repeated passes over the same area, with some adjustments to the wings and blades with each successive pass.

The Jordan's natural advantage over digging equipment that does not ride on the rails is the uniformity and stability afforded by the guiding tracks and the machine's relatively heavy weight. This benefit is especially valuable when plowing or ditching on curved track, as the Jordan can easily maintain a consistent profile. A late-era Jordan Type A weighs about 130,000 pounds, which means it is unlikely to be disturbed by normal ditching duties. The blades are made of extremely tough manganese alloy steel, and are resistant to breakage. Like the *Titanic*, however, the Jordan is not invincible, and the operator must know the limits of his machine. An efficient operator will let the Jordan do its work, allowing a reasonable margin of safety, without being overly cautious. One thing the Jordan is not suited to tackle is large rocks. These are likely to damage the machinery and are best removed before the spreader is set to work.

The early Jordan Spreaders didn't have a protective cab for the crew. Later machines had a small centrally situated cab. Eventually the cab was enlarged and moved forward to give the operator a

On March 23, 1973, a Soo Line Jordan has its wing extended and lowered into position, ready to clear out a ditch along the right-of-way. It is a traditional air-actuated machine dating from the steam era. Some railroads still use Jordans despite the development of more modern equipment. *John Gruber*

better working environment and improved visibility. The four models of spreaders built in later years were the *Standard*, a relatively small machine discontinued in the 1960s; the *Roadmaster*, which was a little larger; the Type A Jordan; and the Type J Jordan. One of the biggest changes in the basic design of the Jordan Spreader was the introduction of hydraulics in the 1950s. Still, even after hydraulics were offered, Jordan continued to build the older pneumatic style of machines. In the world of modern track machinery, where electrical and hydraulic control are the norm, an air-controlled machine seems terribly primitive.

4

Surfacing Equipment

Constructing, maintaining, and improving the surface condition of the tracks is the job of specially designed surfacing equipment. They include tie machines, spike inserters, rail heaters, tampers, and ballast regulators. These are the machines that put the ties, fasteners, and rail in place, and gauge, level, and even out the running surface track.

Inspection and Preparation

Railroads often schedule tie replacement in conjunction with surfacing activities, such as tamping and ballast renewal. Ties are designed to last at least 20 years under normal conditions, and it's not unusual for them to survive 40 years or more in regular service. While the ties last a long time, they don't last forever. When ties begin to disintegrate, they lose their ability to hold spikes and/or fasteners properly and keep the track in gauge. Tie spacing and the number of good ties for a given section of track are central factors in classifying track and determining maximum speeds. Every tie need not be in tip top shape for track to function properly. Ties are often replaced one at a time by a tie gang working with a host of small machines, but are sometimes replaced en masse by gigantic automated track machines, or by simply installing new track in sections or panels.

Looking like an army of gigantic mechanical insects heading off to work, Wisconsin Central tie inserter/extractors and tie cranes work along the Ladysmith Subdivision in September 2000. The machine in front is a tie inserter/extractor.

In the old days, removing rotten ties required jacking the tracks up with portable hand jacks, digging the ballast away from the tie with shovels, and forcing the tie out using long steel rods and specially designed tie tongs. What took a half an hour or more to accomplish by hand now can be done by machine in a matter of seconds.

independently controlled, the machines work together as part of a highly coordinated team. Every machine has a specific assigned task that must be performed in a predetermined order in conjunction with the other equipment.

Tie work is often done as part of a line rehabilitation, so the tie gang will usually work over the same section of track for days at a time until the job is complete. Whenever possible, a section of track will be taken out of service and the authority to use the tracks is handed over to the track gang to allow them to work uninterrupted for as much time as possible. Since tie work disturbs the track structure, it is preferable to have each stage of the job completed as quickly as possible before trains are allowed to operate on the track again. The work may be accomplished in stages, and if trains need to use a section of track before it has been brought back up to go standards, "slow orders" may be assigned over the repaired section. This is especially true where complicated surfacing work, such as ballast cleaning, undercutting, and other work to the roadbed is being done in conjunction with tie work. This

complex track overhaul requires the tracks to settle properly before trains are permitted to operate at top speeds.

A Day Out with the Gang

By the nature of the work that is being done, the warmer months are the preferred time of year for tie and rail maintenance in many areas, especially those afflicted by tough winter weather. The tie gangs usually operate during normal working hours, morning to evening on weekdays, in order to take full advantage of daylight. In the morning, a tie gang is brought to the track machines by a company bus. The machines are typically stored overnight out of the way on sidings when they are not in use. It is desirable to get the machines off the main tracks and passing sidings, so they will often be stored on lightly used, sometimes poorly maintained tracks, which are kept in place at strategic locations along a line for just such work, as well as for setting out damaged cars.

At the start of each workday, the foreman and supervisors discuss a plan of action, and the machine operators make sure their machines are in good order and stocked with the necessary supplies. Before the gang can go to work, the dispatcher has to be contacted for permission. Sometimes a train or two may need to get over the section of track before work can begin; other times the gang can get track authority right away. Once proper authority has been received, the machines proceed out of the siding and run down the line to the spot where work is to begin. This parade of equipment looks something like an army of giant mechanical insects marching off to war. Often there is some duplication in the types of machines in the parade, as two or three of one type might be spaced apart to speed up the work. By the time the machines have arrived at the work site, tie and rail trains will have laid out the appropriate materials, such as ties, tie plates, spikes, rails, and fasteners. If you see fresh materials along a line, this is a pretty good clue that work is in progress or about to take place.

On track that uses traditional wooden ties and spikes, spike pullers and rail anchor removers will come along and free all rail fastenings from ties scheduled for removal. Likewise, on larger sections, where the rail is to be replaced, fasteners are removed from all the ties on the specified section. Once the fasteners are out of the way, tie extractors, tie cranes, and tie inserters come along and remove and replace the defective ties. In some situations, a backhoe can be used to replace ties, but this is not efficient for large jobs. After the ties and rails have been worked on, the track must be regauged and respiked into place, and rail anchors must be reattached as well. On a modern gang, there are machines to do each and every one of these tasks. When the basic track has been re-assembled, new ballast is dumped, and the track is surfaced using ballast regulators and tampers, along with other equipment. If the surface of the track was in good shape prior to the tie and rail work, then simply tamping may be all that's necessary; if not, the tracks will require alignment as well. Lining is done by specialized tampers, described later on. At the end of the day, the machines proceed to the nearest siding and tie up for the evening.

In some situations, such as on heavily used single-track lines, it is not possible to give a track gang more than a few hours at a time to do their work. In these cases, the gang is limited in the amount of work it can accomplish, and the workers must maximize the use of their time. The gang will zip in to place, get the job done, and then zip out again as quickly as it can before its track time expires. A dispatcher cannot run trains until all the machines are safely out of the way and he has received a report describing any slow orders that may be placed on the track. Occasionally work is delayed if a machine breaks down. Since the machines work together in assembly line fashion,

A typical tie crane features a short wheelbase and a long, hydraulically controlled arm with a claw at the end for gripping ties. Several of the ties below the crane have been recently replaced, which is evident by the missing ballast around the ends of the ties.

A Nordco spike inserter pauses between jobs on the Wisconsin Central. This spiker, like most modern track machines, is powered by a diesel engine. The spike driving machinery is operated hydraulically.

one broken machine can "tie up" the whole process (no pun intended).

Spike Pullers

Automated spike pulling machines have made the task of spike removal must faster and easier. A typical spike puller is a relatively small,

self-propelled machine with a welded steel frame. It has a seat and controls for the operator controls, but it is typically an open-air machine, so that the operator can be as close to the work as possible. Usually there is a roof to protect the operator, and a tarpaulin can be draped over the machine to form a tent in case of rain. Spike pulling is serious work, and the puller is not aimed at operator comfort. A spike puller has a particularly awkward look to it that makes it seem like an erector set project gone awry. It lacks symmetry, and doesn't have any metal sheathing to disguise the machinery, which is all exposed to the air on the platform. Most modern spike pullers have two heads that allow them to remove pairs of spike simultaneously. A normal arrangement is for one spike to be taken out from each side of the rail. The removal carriage is hydraulically operated, and consists of a tapered guide with small wheels designed to keep it properly positioned over the rail. The puller jaw is made of very strong alloyed steel that is resistant to damage from the act of spike pulling. The operator uses the controls to direct the carriage jaw to pull the spikes out of the tie. Modern machines are equipped with computers that can be programmed with a pattern to assist the operator in locating and removing spikes as quickly as possible. The carriage can be adjusted up and down, left and right, and forward and backward to center the puller claw over the spike.

Spike pullers are usually set up to work on the left or right side of the track. Depending on the type of job being performed, it is common to see two or more spike pullers working together. Since a tie gang needs to remove all the spikes on a single tie in order to extract it from the track structure, spike pullers are usually paired up, each one working on one side of the track. Often more than two spikes are on each tie plate to hold the rail in place. Anchor spikes are used to secure the tie plate and don't actually come in contact with the rail.

Harsco Track Technologies manufactures a typical dual-action spike puller, the Model W113 Series E. It is just under 12 feet long (11.83 feet), 93 inches wide, 94 inches tall, and uses a 9-foot, 4-inch wheelbase. The machine normally comes with a roof over the operator controls, and a built-in turntable assists with rapid deployment and easy reversal. With these features it weighs 5,380 pounds. Harsco's spike puller is powered by a 42-horsepower diesel engine that operates at 2,800 rpm (very fast compared with diesel locomotive engines, which normally operate at just one-third that speed) and uses a hydraulic propulsion system with a four-wheel roller chain drive. The main hydraulic system has a working pressure of 3,000 psi.

This mechanized tie relaying machine is designed to rehabilitate concrete ties and welded rail simultaneously. It picks up the old rail and ties as it lays down new track, working in a continuous unbroken operation. Built in 1977, this CANAC machine is working on Metro-North at Green's Farms, Connecticut, on July 17, 1999. *Patrick Yough*

Opposite top
A detailed view of the spike feed chutes on a Nordco spiker. The spikes drop in the jaw by gravity and are driven in the tie with a swift strike from a hydraulically powered ram.

Opposite bottom
As mechanical jaws hold the spike in place, the ram will drive the spikes straight into the tie. An automatic spike driver takes the place of men with heavy mallets that would hammer a spike in manually.

The operator station on the Model W113 Series E has a padded swiveling chair with armrests that gives the operator good visibility of the working area. The controls consist of joysticks that enable the operator to direct the spike pulling carriages, and move the machine backward and forward. Since the spike puller must be able to line up perfectly with the spikes, it is important to have accurate slow speed control. Braking is accomplished with a standard foot pedal arrangement. The brakes themselves are adjustable shoe treads that contact one wheel on each axle. Since the machine has a maximum travel speed of only 26 miles per hour, braking is designed for aligning the spike pulling heads, rather than for coming to a smooth swift stop from high speed.

Harsco's Model W134 Series A is a bigger spike puller. It carries two operators and is designed to remove two spikes at a time from *both*

Safe working practices are very important when working on a railroad. When one track is closed to traffic for a steel gang, the other may be open, though trains must proceed at reduced speed through the work site. Here a Kershaw Kribber-Adzer and Grove crane wait for a westbound train to pass before resuming work on the track.

sides of the track simultaneously, eliminating the need for two spike pullers working in tandem. It is set up to allow either operator to drive the machine and position it over the ties. The puller jaws can be adjusted independently of the machine, which is necessary to allow both operators to do their work without interfering with the other. The machine is 12.62 feet long, 102 inches wide, and 112.5 inches tall, and it rides on an 8-foot, 4-inch wheelbase. Its engine is significantly more powerful than that on the W113 Series E, capable of generating 80 horsepower and working at 2,500 rpm. Unlike the single-operator machine, this one only has two-wheel drive.

Tie Extractors and Inserters

Prior to mechanization, replacing ties was a slow, labor-intensive business. After the spikes were removed, the tracks were jacked up using hand jacks. Long iron rods and tie tongs were used to leverage the tie loose and pull it out of place. Often a fair amount of digging was needed to free the tie from its spot. Those days are long gone, thanks to automatic tie extractors and inserters. Now ties can be replaced mechanically as fast as seven per minute with these highly specialized machines.

A full range of tie extractor/inserters are available, ranging from lightweight machines designed for simple jobs, to massive tie-laying machines designed to rehabilitate whole sections of mainline quickly. Several different companies produce these types of machines. A typical smaller machine used by track gangs that need to replace ties intermittently will be just 14 or 15 feet long, self-propelled, and controlled by a single operator. Since a smaller tie extractor usually works on tracks that will be placed back in service shortly after it is finished, the machine has to interfere as little as possible with the overall track structure. In order to remove a tie, the machine clamps on to the rails, and lifts the track slightly with hydraulic jacks. A hydraulically controlled telescoping boom then grips the tie from the end and pulls it out. Since ties can become angled, the boom is able to rotate right or left 10 to 20 degrees off axis from a hypothetical perpendicular in order to grab any wayward ties. The boom must also be able to lift as high as 25 degrees above the track plane, and drop

up to 15 degrees below the track plane to extract the tie from below the rails. This process involves an enormous amount of force. Even a relatively lightweight tie machine, such as Harsco's 925 Tie Inserter/Remover, will apply 39,000 pounds of lifting force to the track, and as much as 19,000 pounds of extracting force on the tie.

Larger tie extracting machines use additional tools to speed up the extracting process. For example, Harsco's RMC305 Series A TKO Tie Remover/Inserter has an optional piece of equipment

that pushes the tie from the end opposite the boom. Since some ties can become bound and difficult to extract, this device applies an addition 10,000 pounds of force, which is usually enough to get even the most stubborn ties moving.

New ties are inserted with the same type of equipment that was used to extract them. The tracks are lifted, and the boom grips the new tie and slides it into place. To facilitate the process, some machines use an adjustable arm to guide the tie underneath the rails.

Tie Cranes

A tie crane works in conjunction with the tie inserter, lifting new ties that have been placed along the right-of-way, and laying them perpendicularly across the tracks for the tie inserter to grab hold of. A tie crane may also pull a small trailer with new ties on it. Tie cranes are also used to stack old ties after they have been removed.

A typical small self-propelled tie crane is a relatively lightweight piece of machinery. They weigh in the vicinity of 7 to 9 tons, and feature a or three people to operate. One person runs the machine and applies spikes to one side of the track, while another operator applies spikes to the other side; the third person supplies the spike chutes with fresh spikes. Although a spike driving machine appears awkward and looks quite complex, its function and operation are actually quite simple. Like other small track machines, a spike driver is self-propelled, with a small diesel engine. A dual-headed machine has a pair of hydraulically or air-powered spike driving rams that insert the spikes into the ties. One operator moves the machine forward, centering it over a tie. The machine tightly grips the track with rail clamps, and mechanical gauging equipment ensures the rails are separated to the precise width. Claws on both sides of the machine, sometimes called "nippers," hold the tie in place, making sure it is tight to the rail, and then both operators begin inserting spikes by directing spike holding clamps to predesignated holes in the tie plate and striking them with powerful automatic rams. Chutes automatically feed fresh spikes into the clamps. These spike drivers take less time to accomplish their tasks than it takes to read about it.

The spike drivers are operated with a mixture of joystick and push-button controls to drive the machine and direct the spiking heads. On most dual-headed machines, either operator may drive the machine. This gives maintenance crews great flexibility in assigning equipment. Some jobs do not require dual spiking and only need one rail spiked in place. In these cases, only one side of the machine is in use, so it would be restrictive if the machine could only be driven from one side or the other.

Harsco's *Zapper* Spike Driver, Model RMC300C1, is a typical modern spike driving machine. It is 24 feet, 4 inches long; 8 feet, 6 inches wide; and 9 feet, 9 inches tall. It weighs about 13 tons. It has a 15-foot wheelbase, and places the driving heads and operators at the center of the machine, very close to rail level. The propulsive, electrical, and hydraulic equipment are located at the rear of the machine. It is capable of a working speed up to 10 miles per hour, and travels at a top speed of 23 miles per hour.

A member of the BNSF steel gang working at Pepin, Wisconsin, attaches a roller transport device to a section of welded rail. The specially equipped Pettibone crane will transfer the rail from the drainage ditch to the track center in preparation for installation.

remarkable short wheelbase, often just 6 feet long. The crane itself can rotate 360 degrees on a center axis, and may be able to reach as far as 25 feet from the center of the track. In order to lift a typical wooden or concrete tie, the crane usually has a lifting capacity of 800 to 1,000 pounds. It may be equipped with locking rail clamps to keep it from tipping over when lifting heavy loads that are far from the center of the track.

Spike Inserters

Spike inserters, sometimes called spike drivers, come in a variety of different formats. A typical machine used for tie jobs would be a moderately sized dual-headed spike driver that requires two

Steel Gangs

A steel gang is the crew responsible for rail maintenance, realignment, and replacement. Like a tie gang, a steel gang travels together around a railroad to perform specialized jobs. It uses many of the same machines as the tie gang, as well as a few others, such as rail preheaters. One of the most common jobs for a steel gang is replacing welded rail on curves. The friction and pressure placed on the rails is much greater on curves, and

The Pettibone crane is one of 20 maintenance machines working with the BNSF steel gang at Pepin in September 2000. The tie crane slides the section of welded rail from the side of the track to the track center. This section of rail is roughly 1,500 feet long and weighs about 140 pounds per yard.

as a result curved track tends to wear much more quickly. On heavily graded lines especially, it takes a real beating compared to level tangent track. Wheels scrape and grind through curves, shaving away at the inside of the railhead, causing gauge widening and rail imperfections that hinder locomotive performance. This can result in track degradation, and could potentially cause a derailment if left unchecked.

A steel gang may use between 15 and 20 machines. While many of the machines have very specific functions, the men operating them are often trained to work with different types of machinery. This versatility and cross-training offers several advantages. It gives the crew members the chance to do different jobs, which keeps them from getting bored by doing the same fairly repetitive task day in and day out. It also gives each worker a clearer understanding of what the gang as a whole is doing. If every person on the

Rolling along at speeds of 1 to 2 miles per hour, Holley Engineering's spike reclaimer has large magnetic wheels on both sides to pick up spikes and rail anchors along the right-of-way after they have been removed by a spike puller.

Following the spike reclaimer, a machine fills the old spike holes with an epoxy chemical compound to prevent decay in the holes, and to give the new spikes a solid hold when they are inserted.

A Job for a BNSF Steel Gang

In September 2000, a Burlington Northern Santa Fe (BNSF) steel gang was given two repair jobs on the same stretch of the No. 1 track (westbound mainline) a few miles east of Pepin, Wisconsin. The track is the former Chicago, Burlington & Quincy mainline along the Mississippi River, connecting Chicago and the Twin Cities. This line was once the raceway of Burlington's famous streamlined *Zephyrs*. Today it is a key component of BNSF's principal Chicago-Pacific Northwest Corridor. While this section of track no longer handles passenger service, it is a busy freight line, accommodating up to 50 freight trains a day. To move this number of trains, most of the line between Savanna, Illinois, and Minneapolis is equipped with double track and directional signaling. When maintenance is performed, one track is taken out of service, and all traffic uses the remaining track. The dispatcher, who is located in a large control center in Fort Worth, Texas, has to "fleet" trains through the work area, using crossovers on either side to get trains from one track to the other. Although the one track remains open to traffic, trains must communicate with the official overseeing the track maintenance before proceeding through the work zone; once they receive permission, the trains are allowed to proceed at reduced speed. Since the gang is working with loud machinery and is focused on the assigned task, the workers may not see a train sneaking up on them on the opposing track. Lookouts are stationed to sound air horns when a train is in sight.

This particular steel gang was equipped with an arsenal of about 20 different machines, arranged in the order in which they would be needed. The gang set out to work on the two jobs simultaneously. One job was to replace a length of continuous welded rail (CWR) near the village of Pepin; the other was a "gauging job," which required regauging a section of rail on an S curve a few miles west (geographically northwest) of town. Since the two jobs involved similar work and were very close to one another, they could be undertaken simultaneously, with machinery going from one to the next.

In anticipation of the rail replacement, a BNSF rail train laid down a section of CWR in the drainage ditch on the north side of the No. 1 track (westbound mainline). This was an adequate place to store the rail out of the way until it was ready to be installed, but the rail had to be properly positioned between the tracks before installation. The rail also needed to be dragged to precisely the right spot along the line. A 1,500-foot-long section of CWR is extremely heavy and can only be moved by machinery. The job of moving the rail

gang knows what everyone else is supposed to do, it makes their working together as a team more productive and efficient. The flexibility to assign crew members to different machines allows the gang to be easily split up to take on smaller jobs, and it alleviates potential scheduling problems if someone in the gang is unable to work.

The dual-purpose Kershaw Kribber-Adzer cleans excess ballast around the ties to facilitate rail laying, and reprofiles a precision tie plate seat on the tie. The machine is supported by rail on one side and by Caterpillar treads on the other.

was left to a former Santa Fe Pettibone Hyrail crane, equipped with a specialized rotating boom, and fitted with a roller attachment for moving rail. The Pettibone set up at the east end of the rail segment. A man on the ground assisted the Pettibone operator with fitting the roller attachment to the rail. Once it was in place, the Pettibone lifted the rail out of the ditch and swung it over to the center of the track. It did this by leveraging one end of the rail in place, and as the crane ran down the track it slid the rail over from the ditch to the track center as it went. After placing the new rail between the two outer rails, the Pettibone dragged it into position. The rest of the job was to be completed with machines that were working on the gauging project.

Further down the line, at the second site, the gauging job was already under way. Here the rail sits in the middle of the S curve. Heavy wear had broadened the gauge of the track slightly through the curve, and the rail needed to be completely removed, and then put back, regauged, and refastened into place.

The entire entourage of track equipment working on the gauging project passed over the section of rail and set up at the far west end of the work site. Since the machines are lined up in the order of the job they do, and since they will proceed to the rail-replacement project as they complete their work on this job, the gang must start at the west end and work east; otherwise, every machine will have to wait for the entire gauging job to be

finished before it can move on to the rail replacement. A good maintenance planner has to think out every step of the maintenance process to get maximum use out of the gang.

The first machines to work the regauging job are an anchor remover and a spike puller, both built by Nordco. They proceed along the track clearing spikes and anchors from the rail and dropping them on the ground. A Holley Engineering Model 58-10 Spike Reclaimer follows closely be-

hind, picking up the metal parts that have been dumped. This clever machine alleviates the need for workers to pick up the discarded spikes and anchors by hand, and effectively allows one man to do the job of many. Built in April 1995, the model used on this job weighs 17,500 pounds. The Holley spike reclaimer employs two large electromagnetic wheels, one on each side of the tracks, to pick up spikes, anchors, bolts, and just about any other small bits of steel from along the ballast.

A Grove crane re-lays and regauges a segment of welded rail. This is precision work and the most important part of the gauging work. The whole purpose of the job is to put the tracks back into gauge, which may mean adjusting the rail by fractions of an inch.

A Teleweld rail warmer is a crucial piece of equipment when laying continuous welded rail, as the rail must be heated to the proper temperature before installation. Rows of propane heaters on the machine heat the rail after it has been laid down and gauged, but before it is anchored in place.

This Fairmont Tamper Anchor-Boxer is used to automatically clip anchors to the rails. Rail anchors are especially important on welded rail to keep it from sliding lengthwise along the tracks. The bin full of new anchors is to the right of the operator controls.

These steel parts are dumped into a V-shaped chute, from where they are deposited into a bin that sifts out dirt and debris from the steel. The steel is transferred to a constantly rotating cylinder that sorts the parts, which are then dropped by a conveyor into canisters on the back of the machine. A stash of empty canisters is stored on the front of the 58-10 Spike Reclaimer.

Next in line is a machine that squirts an epoxy compound into the spike holes in the ties. Two men walking along behind the machine squirt the greenish colored epoxy compound into the holes using pressurized applicators on the end of hoses. This compound prevents decay and fills up the holes so that the new spikes grip properly when they are inserted into the old holes. Without this, the spikes might not hold well. Imagine pulling an old rusty nail out of a board and then putting a new nail back in the same hole. Unless something is done to reduce the size of the hole, the nail may

Moving forward, the ballast regulator pushes and spreads the ballast with its plow. The plow can also be used to draw ballast toward the track center when the regulator runs in the opposite direction.

Right
A ballast regulator works the Wisconsin Central at Hawkins, Wisconsin. Ballast regulators usually have three sets of tools for moving, sculpting, and manicuring ballast: the plows, the ballast box, and the rotary broom.

not hold very well. Considering the thousands of pounds of pressure per square inch that will be placed on the spikes holding this rail in place, the new spikes must have a good hold, or there will be serious consequences. The epoxy does the trick.

The rail is now ready to be regauged. It is cut manually with a high-speed rotary saw. Another Pettibone tractor, this one running with its rubber tires on the ballast, lifts the rail off the tie plates and places it on the ties at the center of the track. Workers then walk along and manually lift the tie plates off the ties with rods and lay them in the ballast. These tie plates will be reused to seat the rail. Next along is a self-propelled cribber-adzer that is supported by a set of steel wheels on one side, which ride on the rail that is still intact, and on the other by Caterpillar treads. As the machine goes along, the operator brushes away excess ballast from the crib between the ties, and then using a computer-controlled adzer, cuts a precision tie plate seat on the top of the tie to ensure the re-gauged rail sits properly.

A large Grove crane then lifts the rail and lays it back in place. The Grove operator has the one job in the steel gang that requires a specialist, and only a few men on the gang are trained to operate it. Aligning the rail must be done with precision accuracy, and this task takes a little

The ballast box sculpts the ballast, giving it the desired angle for proper drainage.

more time than the rest of the procedures. Several men follow along putting tie plates under the rail as it is positioned. Getting the tie plates to seat properly beneath the rail often requires a few whacks with a sledgehammer. The rail segment is not reconnected at this time; this procedure must wait until later.

Once the rail is seated, a spike driver comes along to fix the rail in place. This is just a preliminary spiking, and another spiker will follow later to add more spikes. A tamper then shores up the ballast, and it is followed by a Teleweld rail warmer. The rail warmer is a fairly large two-piece machine that carries a large propane tank. It has rows of heaters that raise the temperature of the rail before it is fixed in place. Rail warming is a crucial operation to avoid future problems caused by rail expansion. The rail is brought up to 95 degrees Fahrenheit, which is the designated installation temperature for a rail on this line. When the rail is at the proper temperature, remaining fasteners are attached, including more spikes and rail anchors. The anchors are laid by a pair of anchor applicators that operate in tandem with each other. Two machines are used so that the anchors are applied as quickly as possible; since rail anchors are designed to keep the rail from sliding lengthwise along the ties, the rail must be anchored in place before it cools.

As each set of machines completes its task on the gauging job, it proceeds down the line to the rail replacement job, where most of the same steps are repeated, except a new rail is installed instead of regauging the old one. The entire procedure for both jobs is accomplished relatively quickly. This gang is highly experienced so the work moves along at a steady pace with few difficulties or interruptions. All the while the gang is working, BNSF is rolling mile-long freight trains by.

Ballast Regulators

The ballast regulator is a common but versatile piece of modern railway maintenance equipment. While many track maintenance machines are limited to specifically defined tasks, the ballast regulator, like the Jordan Spreader, is an adaptable machine. It is designed to move and sculpt ballast, but it can be used for ditch digging, brush removal, plowing snow (see chapter 7), and assisting with laying cable. A basic ballast regulator is controlled by a single operator, who drives the machine and oversees its operation. Most ballast regulators have three primary tools for working with ballast: plow blades that can be lowered over the tracks; adjustable ballast boxes on either side of the machine; and a rotating brush.

After rail and tie maintenance, ballast cleaning, undercutting, or any other work that disturbs, removes or alters the track and roadbed, a ballast train will lay down fresh ballast on the tracks. Depending on the nature of the work that had been completed and the type of ballast train used, ballast may be laid either to the side of the rails or between them. In order for ballast to be most effective, it needs to be packed around, between, and beneath the ties and sculpted to the desired profile. Heaps of ballast alongside the tracks or sitting atop the ties don't help the condition of the track. A ballast regulator helps put ballast in its desired place. It often works as part of a surfacing gang that includes tamping equipment and other machines.

Regulators usually feature two angled, double-sided plow blades at the front, which can be used to move ballast backward or forward. The blades are angled to face away from the regulator. They are adjustable vertically and can work together or separately. Using the blades, the regulator can plow ballast off the track, drag ballast from the side of the track to the center, or even move loads of ballast from one side of the track to the other. Plowing is relatively straightforward. For ballast that is set on top of the ties between the rails and needs to be spread over the track, the operator simply lowers the blades to the desired height above the ties and drives forward over the ballast, spreading it across the tracks, filling in gaps, and evening it out. This is one of the simplest plow functions. A more complicated task involves moving ballast from one side of the rails to the other or to the track center. If a pile of ballast is set to the right of the rails and needs to be centered on the track, the operator drives forward past the ballast pile, stops, and lowers the plow blade on the right side, keeping the left-hand blade raised. He then reverses the regulator and drives back over the pile of ballast, drawing it toward the center of the track. Depending on the size of the pile, the type of stone, and the amount of ballast to be moved, this procedure may have to be repeated more than once. To move the same ballast to the left side of the track, another pass is required, essentially performing the opposite procedure: the regulator moves forward with the left-hand blade down and the right one raised, pushing the ballast to the left. Using this technique, a regulator operator can get ballast to where it is needed most and distribute it evenly all along the track.

The regulator operator sits in a central control cabin with windows on all sides to give him a good, clear view of the tracks and the action. Some regulators have two sets of controls (one for the right plow blades and one for the left) so that the operator can stay close to whichever set of blades he is working with, providing a better sense of control.

In this view, the regulator has its ballast box retracted and plows lifted while the broom is deployed. The broom rotates quickly to sweep excess ballast off the tops of the ties.

The ballast box assemblies on the sides of the regulator are adjustable. They can move laterally outward from the side of the machine, and pivot up and down to adjust the angle. As the regulator rolls along, the boxes are used to draw ballast on the side of the track closer to the centerline, and they sculpt and contour the ballast to the desired profile. A typical ballast profile on a lightweight single track line includes a 14-inch shoulder where the stone is level with the tops of the ties. Beyond the shoulder, the ballast should slope down at an angle that drops 1 inch for every 3 inches out from the track center. To achieve this profile, the regulator operator sets the ballast box to the desired extended position from the machine and angles it to the ground. He pulls the ballast into place by dragging the box along. This sometimes can be accomplished with just one well-planned pass over a given section of track, but several passes may be required, depending on the skill of the operator, the capabilities of the regulator, and the amount of ballast that needs to be moved. Ideally, modern regulators should be able to accomplish most jobs in a single pass, but in reality this is not always practical.

After ballast has been moved, spread, and contoured using the plow and the ballast boxes, piles of stone are left on top of the ties. In order to clean off the ties and finish the job properly, the regulator is equipped with a spinning broom to remove stray stones and debris. The broom is composed of a rotating bar with multiple sets of five or six spokes radiating from it. One common type of regulator has 19 sets of spokes, five sets on the outside of each rail and nine in between. The spokes wear down rapidly, and they are usually made from an easily replaceable material such as used air-brake hoses. There is always a plentiful supply of these around a railroad, which makes them ideal spoke material. The hoses may be filled with wire cables to make them more effective in moving debris off the tracks. The broom spins rapidly as the regulator rolls along, kicking stones and debris off the ties, making for a clean, nicely manicured right-of-way. Rubber flaps are set up around the broom to keep rocks from escaping the regulator. Often a few stray ones will get loose, flying 20 to 30 feet away, so it isn't safe to stand close to a working regulator. By the nature of the work it does, a ballast regulator stirs up a lot of dust. A machine plowing a pile of ballast will appear as a miniature dust storm raging along the tracks. Because of this, the best time for a regulator to do its work is when it is raining or when the ground is still wet from rain.

A ballast regulator at work is an amazing sight, but it is equally amazing to see a nice freshly regulated section of track. Before the ballast regulator arrives, track has a remarkably unkempt appearance. There are piles of stones heaped left, right, and center. The ends of the ties are obscured by ballast, and rocks are sitting all over the tops of the ties. After the ballast regulator makes its passes over the track, plowing, sculpting, and sweeping the stones, the right-of-way has a finished, polished appearance that exemplifies good-looking track.

Several different manufacturers produce ballast regulators, including Knox Kershaw of Montgomery, Alabama; Nordco, of Milwaukee, Wisconsin; and Harsco Track Technologies. In 2001, Knox Kershaw offered three ballast regulator models: the KBR825, KBR850, and KBR900. As one might expect from the model numbers, the KBR825 is the smallest in this family of machines and the KBR900 is the largest. The KBR825 is intended to accomplish each of its basic functions in a single pass. It has a one-pass transfer plow designed to move ballast from one side of the track to the other. Its side-mounted ballast wings are 36 inches wide and controlled hydraulically from the cab. The broom is also hydraulically controlled, and it has an adjustable

Many small track maintenance machines have built-in turntables that allow a single operator to turn the machine around. This Burlington Northern regulator is being turned in front of the Cascade Tunnel at Cascade Summit, Washington. *Tom Kline*

deflector to protect against flying rocks. This deflector can be positioned as the ballast regulator moves through complicated track arrangements. The machine is powered by a Cummins engine and is designed for a travel speed of 30 miles per hour when it is not working. The KBR850 is slightly larger, and it has greater ballast moving capabilities than the KBR825. Its wings reach up 13 feet, 6 inches from the track center. The KBR900 is Kershaw's largest model. Its simple, durable construction is designed to achieve the work as safely and efficiently as possible. Among its special features is a tilting operator's cab, which can be adjusted to give the machine operator the best possible view of the tracks. The plow wings are designed to snap off the machine if it strikes an obstruction while working. This is a safety feature similar to a collapsing steering wheel column in an automobile, intended to preserve the safety of the operator. The bolt holding the wing in place is set up as the weakest point of the whole assembly. In this way the bolt breaks rather than the wing or more substantial parts of the regulator. If the wing snaps off, the operator can reinstall it right away, using a new bolt to hold it in place.

Nordco calls its ballast regulator the Ground Hog. By using a rear-mounted engine, the regulator affords the operator a clear, unobstructed forward view of the tracks. Its four-wheel, hydrostatic propulsion is designed for a travel speed of 35 miles per hour. Like the Kershaw regulators, the Ground Hog is designed for single-pass operations, thus saving time by reducing the need for driving back and forth over the same section of track. The Ground Hog's wings reach 14 feet from the track centers.

In 1986, the Tamper Corporation, one of Harsco's predecessors, introduced its C-series line of modular track maintenance equipment. The C-series line was aimed at standardizing the use of basic components employed by different types of machines. (This standardization practice is nothing new to railroading; the Pennsylvania Railroad began standardizing its locomotive designs back in the 1860s.) Tamper standardized its designs to help reduce the cost of machine production and maintenance in order to counter the increased costs of implementing advancing equipment technology, among other expenses. Tamper's modular approach to construction reduced the time required to produce the machines, limited the number of parts it needed to

Previous page
An example of a classic tamping machine, Pioneer Valley Railroad's tamper rests at the shop in Westfield, Massachusetts.

stock, and simplified operator training. Tamper's C154BR ballast regulator, for example, shared components with its cribbing machines and track tampers. The C154BR not only employed a modular design but also had a greater capacity than earlier machines, and its specifications were intended to match the capacity of tampers in the C-Series. Since ballast regulators often work in tandem with tampers, it is important that they do their work at about the same rate so that one machine does not fall way behind the work of the other. Some 15 years after it was introduced, the C154BR regulator is still produced by Harsco.

A modern C154BR regulator is 31 feet, 8 inches long; a little more than 10 feet wide; and 10 feet, 10 inches tall. The machine normally weighs about 56,000 pounds. It has a four-wheel-drive propulsion system powered by a 200-horsepower Cummins 6BTA 5.9 diesel engine. It is capable of a travel speed of 50 miles per hour. The front plow is 10 feet wide and is intended for single-pass ballast transferal. The hydraulic side wings extend 12 feet, 6 inches from the track center. The ballast boxes have a 1.75-cubic-yard capacity for moving stone. The hydraulic system is powered by a variable displacement pump that operates at 2,000 to 2,500 psi. The broom is mounted on the rear of the machine, a standard placement, and may be set to spin in either direction.

Some ballast regulators, such as the Plasser PBR-550, have a built-in ballast hopper, which allows the regulator to carry some of its own ballast. This feature is useful in situations in which the regulator requires additional ballast to do its work properly, but it is inconvenient for the railroad to send in a ballast train. The PBR-500 has a small hopper that carries 6 cubic yards of ballast.

On a large surfacing gang, several ballast regulators may work together to dress a section of track. The number of ballast regulators required depends on the other types of equipment being used. Since the capacity and speed of different makes and models of maintenance machines varies considerably, it is important that machines are matched to one another for greatest efficiency, and to make the most of a given work window. For example, a high-capacity production tamper may be able to work at an average speed of 2 miles an hour, while a single ballast regulator might cover only one-quarter of that distance in the same amount of time. To keep up with the tamper, four or five ballast regulators may be assigned to work together on the same job. In the mid-1980s, Conrail's typical surfacing gang had 55 people working a variety of different jobs, with more than 20 different machines, including six ballast regulators. The task assigned to each ballast regulator would vary depending on its position in

The large Plasser & Theurer production tamper is used by Iarnród Éireann (Irish Rail). European railroads tend to use faster production machines because they have less track time available for maintenance. Amtrak uses similar tampers on its Northeast Corridor for the same reasons.

the gang and the type of work being done. To minimize the amount of set-up time, a single regulator might spend the entire shift just plowing ballast, while another was given the sole task of brooming, even though each machine was fully capable of doing both tasks.

Most ballast regulators, and other types of small track maintenance machines, come equipped with a turntable that allows the machine to rotate and change direction. The turntable is simple to operate. It raises the machine off the wheels, spins it 180 degrees, and sets it back down again. This easy ability to change direction simplifies operations and adds to the ballast regulator's versatility.

Tampers

Where there's a ballast regulator, a track tamper is probably not too far behind. These two machines often work together in rehabilitating track. There are several different basic types of

tampers, and dozens of different models. Tampers can perform three basic functions: track tamping, jacking (or surfacing), and lining, all of which are designed to improve the condition of the tracks. Tamping is the shoring up of the ballast below the ties to improve the support of the track. Jacking involves lifting and vertically aligning the track to even out bumps and other defects. Lining is the lateral alignment of the tracks. When these three features are properly combined and controlled, the result is better-supported tracks that are straighter and more even than they were prior to tamping.

The mechanization of the tamping process has greatly speeded and improved this element of basic railway maintenance. Traditionally all the functions of a tamping machine were performed manually by a track gang. Tamping involved squeezing the ballast up below the ties, one tie at a time, by men with shovels and ballast rods and

lots of elbow grease. Jacking was done with traditional track jacks, and lining was done by groups of men with large iron bars. Measuring the amount of jacking and lining was the responsibility of a track foreman, who eyed up the changes and issued verbal instructions to his crew. The whole process was labor-intensive, imprecise, and slow. The first step toward mechanizing the tamping process came with the introduction of automatic hand tamping tools in the 1930s. Later track-based tamping machines revolutionized track maintenance. Today instead of large gangs of men with bars and shovels, tamping is achieved by sophisticated automated track machines.

How Mechanized Tamping Works

A tamping machine has four pairs of metal tamping tools, each of which does the work once accomplished by two men with a tamping bar. The tamping tools are rods with small paddles, specifically shaped for moving ballast ef-

Opposite top
These three close-up views demonstrate the sequence of the tamping tools. In this first shot, the tamper tools are in the retracted position; they are vibrating slightly.

Opposite bottom
The vibrating action helps liquefy the ballast as the tools are thrust downward by the tamper operator.

fectively. Two pairs of tools bracket the rail on each side of the tie, working similar to a large set of chopsticks, or a pair of pliers. They are designed to push through the surface of the ballast to a designated point below the tie and then squeeze the ballast up under the tie. Several different things must occur at the right time and in the proper sequence for the automated tamping to be properly executed:

To break the surface of the ballast, the tamping tools oscillate back and forth very quickly on the axis of the rods, usually at a rate of about 3,200 vibrations per minute. (To the naked eye it appears that the tamping tools are just shaking, and the subtle oscillation isn't noticeable.) Four three-phase electric motors (one for each pair of tools) create the rapid oscillation, which has the effect of a miniature earthquake when the tools come in contact with the ballast. The oscillation effectively liquefies the ballast, providing the tools with an easy entry to do their work. As the tools are thrust into the ground, they contact a switch when they reach the proper depth (which must be set according to the thickness of the ties). A signal is sent to large hydraulic cylinders that then squeeze the opposing sets of tools together, scrunching the ballast. The combination of the high-frequency oscillation and the scrunching is designed to cause the liquefied ballast to flow under the tie at the desire point. When the scrunching action is complete, the tools are automatically released and

When the tools reach the proper depth, they are automatically squeezed together, forcing ballast upward below the tie.

Dick Gruber of Wisconsin & Southern tamps the yard at Janesville, Wisconsin. This production tamper uses the Delta System for lining and surfacing track.

lifted back into their normal position above the tracks. The whole procedure takes just a few seconds and is known as the Tamp Cycle. The cycle itself has three steps: (1) downfeed, (2) squeeze in, and (3) squeeze out and upfeed. On older tamping machines, the operator had to manually actuate each of the steps; on modern machines, it is all done automatically.

In order to get the best result from this tamping action, the tool has to be carefully set to reach the desired depth below the tie prior to squeezing. If the rods don't go deep enough, the tie will get squeezed instead of the ballast, which damages the tie and fails to tamp the ballast in place. If the tools go too deep, the ballast flows over the tops of the paddles, resulting in a poor tamp that will not produce the desired support. For the best results, the top of the tamping tool paddles should stop about 1/4 to 1/2 inch below the bottom of the tie.

Track tamping theory has evolved from generations of experience. The most useful tamping action is obtained by uplifting the ballast only below the areas near the rail, while the space between the rails should be left alone. The reasons for this are quite practical. The area below the rail requires the most support, and the passage of trains will tend to tamp the ballast below the ties. If ballast is mechanically tamped along the full length of the tie, the ballast below the center of the tie will eventually become compacted with the passage of trains. This is known as a center-bound tie. When a tie becomes center-bound, it no longer provides proper support below the rails and will rock back and forth under the weight of the train. In extreme situations this can actually cause the tie to break in the middle. The same

type of problem can also be caused by over tamping a tie. Normally just a single tamp cycle by an automatic tamper will provide sufficient support to shore up the tracks.

Another factor in the amount and quality of the tamping is the amount of pressure the tools place on the ballast during the "squeeze in" part of the cycle. Under normal conditions, each pair of tools is set to exert a pressure of about 1,000 psi on the ballast. This results in much greater pressure actually being exerted on the tie, especially when all four sets of tools are tamping simultaneously (which is often the case when tamping track). In situations where ballast has become fouled and cemented through deterioration, greater squeezing pressure may be required. Under most circumstances, the pressure is kept below about 1,400 psi, except on some sophisticated modern computerized tampers.

Though tamping a section of damaged track can greatly improve its surface quality, tamping has some limitations, and it is not a panacea for poor track conditions. If the ballast has severely deteriorated, or if there is insufficient ballast, tamping may only prove minimally useful. Likewise, if rails are bent or ties are rotted and cracked, tamping may not help much at all. Tamping alone cannot cure the effects of serious track deterioration. For this reason, track tamping is often performed in conjunction with rail and tie renewal programs, and after fresh ballast has been applied and regulated.

Metal tamping tool paddles are rectangular in shape when new, designed for most efficient ballast adjustment, but even hardened steel has limited durability when repeatedly scraping against stone. The continual thrusting of the metal tools into the ballast causes the paddles to wear down. As the tools wear, efficiency gradually decreases to the point where the tools must be replaced. This point is normally about 30 percent paddle wear. If the tools are allowed to wear much more than this, the quality of the tamping begins to noticeably suffer.

Jacking and Lining

Because simply improving the ballast support without aligning the track will not improve the surface quality, modern mechanical production track tampers usually combine the basic tamping function with jacking and lining. A tamper that does jacking and lining must have a support system to allow the machine to lift up the tracks. This can be accomplished by incorporating a heavy frame superstructure around the jacking and tamping tools, which in effect makes the tamper a rolling bridge that supports the weight of the track structure during jacking. As a result, a

Harsco's Mark IV production tamper is designed for surfacing and lining as well as basic tamping work. Its large truss frame is needed to support the machine when it lifts the track during lining. This sophisticated piece of modern equipment is used on many railroads in the United States.

production tamper—one that does both surfacing and lining work—is a much larger and more substantial piece of equipment than a basic tamping machine that performs only ballast tamping. On some Harsco tampers, such as the ES-TD, the support is accomplished with a torsion beam jacking system. On these machines, the large torsion beam transfers the track support from the rail to the beam.

Automatic jacking is achieved by a gripping device on the tamper that holds onto the rail and hydraulically lifts the track from above. Lining is accomplished by moving the rail laterally while it is being jacked. For the jacking and lining to have a lasting effect, it must be done at the same time as tamping, so that the track's altered position is supported once the jack releases it. Most of these adjustments to the track structure require relatively small movements, yet they must be coordinated with precise accuracy for the track surface and alignment to be markedly improved.

Each tamper producer has developed its own distinctive system for coordinating automated jacking and lining functions. In the late 1950s Tamper developed its Delta System, which is still used today by Harsco Track Technologies. The purpose of surfacing and lining is to remove irregularities in

the track. To do this properly, the tamping machine needs to establish a point of reference from which to work. Tamper's Delta System creates a reference point using a modulated red beam of light that is projected from a designated point in front of the machine, and is received by equipment behind the jacking and tamping equipment. The frequency of the light is modulated to minimize interference from outside light sources. Under most circumstances this system works as intended, although some tamper operators find that the machines can get confused at sunset, when high-intensity, low reddish light interferes with the projector. The Delta System uses basic triangulation principles of geometry to plot the amount of aligning needed in curves while maintaining a consistent reference point above the track.

The basic system for this procedure involves a frame that rolls in front of the tamper and holds the infrared projector. The distances between the projector and the tamper, and between the projector and the tracks remains constant. Typically the projector is set up 120 feet in front of the receiver. A signal is sent by the modulated red-light receiver to the motors that operate the jacks, which depend on the condition of the infrared beam transmitted by the projector. The jacks are equipped

The Mark IV tamper lines and surfaces track by using a clamp that attaches to the rails and lifts the tracks slightly while simultaneously tamping the ballast below the ties.

curve, the outside rail is slightly higher than the inside rail. When a tamper is working, it is extremely important that the desired superelevation is maintained.) There are two receivers at the back of the machine, one monitoring the surfacing beam, the other a cross level beam. Since the receiver is always at the level of the corrected track, the average inputs from the projector are used to maintain the desired superelevation and curvature. Prior to tamping, the tamper moves through the curve, measuring and plotting the average superelevation and curvature on a graph. Using a device called an Auto Graphliner, the tamper operator can make adjustments to the amount of superelevation and curvature that is put into the track by the jacking and lining. This device presents a clear picture to the operator that facilitates corrections to the curve geometry. Once corrections have been made to the plotted graph, the tamper is then ready to start again over the same section of track, implementing the desired corrections while performing its surfacing and lining.

Switch Tampers

A variation on the basic tamper is the switch tamper, which is designed to do tamping on more complicated track arrangements, such as switches and crossings. The primary difference between switch tampers and ordinary tampers is that the operator can laterally adjust the position of the tamping tools, which is very important when working on switches. On ordinary tampers, the heads are fixed in place and cannot be moved laterally.

Smaller tampers working on typical American freight railroads often operate in pairs or groups. On a large surfacing gang, a switch tamper may work ahead of a pair of surfacing and lining tampers, with a chase tamper following behind. While the tampers are performing similar actions, each one is doing a different job. On a smaller gang, there may just be two tampers. The lead machine takes care of the more complicated surfacing and lining functions, but only works every second tie. The chase tamper that follows is a basic tamper that shores up the alternate ties that the lead tamper missed.

Models of Tamping Machines

Harsco's Mark IV tamper is a typical machine used by many American railroads. As a standard feature it incorporates the old Tamper Delta System with a modern computer control system that is simple and easy to use. The computer regulates the machine during its various functions, and also measures, records, and analyzes the condition of the track in preparation for lining curves. It can also be equipped with a laser alignment system in place of the Delta System. The Mark IV is 39.6 feet long,

with a shadow board that interrupts the modulated red-light beam when the jacks have lifted the tracks to the desired height. When the beam is interrupted, the receiver sends a signal to stop lifting. Since all the other elements of the equation are constant, the result should be nicely aligned track. There are actually two sets of projectors, one for the horizontal plane and one for the vertical plane, which set the parameters for surfacing and lining respectively.

The basic principles of this system are easiest to understand when tamping level tangent track; it is more complicated when working with curved track. This is where the triangulation principle comes in. The Delta System uses three-point coordination. To accommodate curved track, the projector is linked to a sensor on the frame above the opposite rail. The sensor is designed to establish a reference plane above the tracks that reflects the angle of cross level in the track resulting from superelevation. (Superelevation is an angle in the plane of the tracks designed to compensate for the effects of centrifugal forces on railway cars as they roll through curves. In a superelevated

A Harsco Mark VI Model 6700 tamper works the Union Pacific mainline in Nebraska on a rainy day in Spring 1999. The Mark VI is a modern production tamper that uses a truss frame for support when lifting track. *John Gruber*

10.5 feet wide, and 10.5 feet tall. It weighs about 60,000 pounds. Among its features is a variable wheelbase that is 317 inches to 360 inches long. This allows for adjustments to improve the stability of the ties that have already been tamped by keeping the rear axle of the tamper close to the tamping heads. It also improves the machine's lifting ability when working on complicated track arrangements. The tamper uses a strong boxed-beam steel frame construction, a trunnion-mounted front-axle suspension system and a fixed rear axle. It is equipped with 16 tamping tools, arranged in the standard pattern of eight opposing pairs. Its hydraulic oscillating vibrators are designed to work at 3,000 vibrations per minute, with a displacement of 3/8 inch. A Cummins 6CTA 8.3 turbocharged diesel engine provides power. The Mark IV has four-wheel-drive propulsion and has a travel speed of 35 miles per hour.

Harsco's Mark VI, Model 6700 is a typical production and switch tamper. It shares many of the same features as the Mark IV. Among its features are laterally adjustable tamping tools that will reach across the width of any normal switch or crossing. Like the Mark IV, the Mark VI is a truss-suspended machine with 16 tamping tools. It is designed to tamp at a rate of 1/2 mile per hour, and has a 45-mile-per-hour travel speed. It can work on tracks as steep as a 6.5 percent incline (that is, a climb of 6 1/2 feet for every 100 traveled), which is much steeper than any mainline American railroad, although some transit lines may have short ramps that approach that amount of gradient. The tamper is 43 feet, 6 inches long and has a fixed 30-foot wheelbase. It weighs 5 tons more than the Mark IV. Its jacking system can grab either the base or the top of the rail.

Plasser-American's model 09-32 Unimat 4S is a massive switch and production tamper intended for complicated tamping jobs at interlockings and junctions, as well as rapid tamping on mainline tangents. The tamper measures 94 feet, 7 inches long; 9 feet, 9 inches wide; and 13 feet, 5 inches tall. It weighs 273,000 pounds. It has a 442-horsepower engine and is designed for a travel speed of 50 miles per hour. It has the ability to lift tracks at three points simultaneously and tamp four rails at the same time. This type of complex production tamper is popular in Europe, where multiple-track mainlines and heavy passenger traffic are the norm. It is also the type of machine used by Amtrak along the Northeast Corridor, where the high volume of traffic mandates frequent maintenance, but where work windows are relatively short to avoid interfering with passenger schedules.

5

Rail Grinding

O ne warm summer evening in 1984, some friends and I had the good fortune to witness a rail grinding train roll through the Amtrak station in Springfield, Massachusetts. The train had been working all day up on "the Hill," the old Boston & Albany mainline in the Berkshires of western Massachusetts. As the train crawled through the station against the current of traffic on the Number 1 track, I inspected the machinery. The grinder consisted of several cars coupled together. On the sides of the machine were stored dozens of circular grinding stones, tools, and related equipment. The grinder was painted an orange-yellow color, but after days and days of hard work, the entire machine was covered in slate-colored dust and grime. Toward the back of the machine, set upon it like a permanent fixture, was a bedraggled track worker. After a long hot humid day grinding track in the Berkshires, he—like the machine he was working with— was totally covered in grime. It seemed that no part of him was free of it. Although I didn't take his photograph as the train rolled by, I will never forget the expression on his face. Exhausted and ambivalent, he was as impassive as a shell-shocked war veteran. He looked like he had seen it all. Once the rail grinder had cleared the mainline, the freight trains, many of which had been held during the day's work, began to roll, one right after another through

A Pandrol-Jackson grinder profiles Delaware & Hudson tracks at West Waterford, New York. Rail grinding is an essential part of maintaining healthy rail conditions by improving the rail profile after excessive wear. *Jim Shaughnessy*

Rail grinding is hard work, and serious business. Properly profiled rail can save a railroad lots of money by extending the rail life and reducing wear to other track components. Grinding heavily traveled lines, particularly in curves, is especially important. Loram grinder No. 6 profiles a curve at Wiermar, Texas, on February 8, 1992. *Tom Kline*

Right
Alert the authorities—the aliens have landed! No, it's just a rail-grinding train at night. All too frequently, concerned citizens alert police and fire departments when they see the nocturnal fireworks of a rail grinder. With as many as 120 grinding stones shaving steel simultaneously, a grinder can be quite a show.

Springfield station. Why, I wondered, was it so important to subject men and machinery to the rigors of rail grinding?

Steel wheels on steel rails is the story of railroading. Yet, steel wheels inflict terrible damage on the rails. Every inch of the way, wheels are fighting the rails that guide them; they grind, flatten, and distort as they roll along. Wheels cause destruction at every point where they contact the rails. It may not be obvious after a single passing of a train, but the damage is there. The more wheels that roll over rails, and the greater the load those wheels support, the more damage is done. The contact between rail and wheel damages the wheels as well, and as the wheel is worn, it proves more and more damaging to the rail. On tangent track, locomotives have a tendency to hunt (travel rhythmically back and forth), which causes unevenness in the rail. Over time, the effect is comparable to traveling on a bumpy dirt "washboard" road. Curved track suffers from additional problems. As wheels take a curve, they place great pressure on the outside rail, grinding away the head and distorting its shape.

On a busy mainline, maintaining healthy rail conditions is very important business. High levels of rail wear leads to a variety of problems that contribute to a general deterioration of the track structure. This wear is also damaging to passing trains and lowers the overall efficiency of the railroad. On traditional lines with jointed rail, it was relatively easy to exchange sections of damaged rail one piece at a time. Steel rails are very expensive,

however, and exchanging them is both costly and time-consuming. On a modern railroad, the costs of changing rail are an even greater concern. Since most modern mainlines employ continuous welded rail, exchanging sections is extremely time-consuming and labor-intensive, and requires the line to be shut down for many hours at a time. Furthermore, the railroads have eliminated superfluous, redundant, and underutilized tracks and facilities, and as a result they have far less mainline today than ever before—not just fewer routes, but less track. Lines that once had double-track mainlines now often are just single track. This one track, using strategically placed passing sidings, carries all the tonnage of the entire line. When the track is out of service, the railroad stops and waits for it to be restored. This scaled-down network, combined with the increases in railroad

Each grinder has its own circular grinding stone. The stones have short useful service lives and must be replaced often to provide an optimum grinding profile. Piles of used grinding stones are stacked along the gangway of a Loram rail grinder at Cashmere, Washington. *Tom Kline*

productivity and the ever-greater amounts of traffic, presents greater problems for routine maintenance. Rail wear is higher, yet less time is available to take the track out of service to correct it. This doesn't mean the railroads are being run into the ground. Instead, modern maintenance programs, including rail grinding, have greatly reduced the amount of time needed for railway maintenance. Rail grinding technology has evolved to actually prevent problems before they happen.

Rail grinding offers a practical solution to rail replacement. It can greatly increase the useful life of rail by improving the rail profile to facilitate a lower wear rate, prevent fatigue, and eliminate surface defects, while controlling damage from wheel hunting. Rail grinding minimizes the destructive forces caused by wheel-rail contact, which in turn limits the damage to other track components. It reduces the accumulation of steel particulates and other dirt that result from high track wear, thus extending the life of ballast. Also, proper rail profiling reduces wear to fasteners and joints. A better rail profile increases efficiency through improved contact between wheel and rail, resulting in lower fuel consumption, a smoother ride, and less noise.

Modern rail grinders use specialized rotary grinding stones, powered by either electric or hydraulic motors, to reprofile worn rail. Various grades of stone are used, the coarsest for the heaviest work, and the finest for finishing work. The life span of the grinding stones is relatively short, typically requiring replacement every two or three hours. Sometimes stones break during grinding and need immediate replacement. The

high frequency of stone replacement requires that the stones be easily removed from the grinders, a procedure that is repeated more than 100 times a day on a large production grinding train.

Each rail grinding train has banks of grinders that are carefully positioned by a computer to obtain the desired profile. Since the purpose of grinding is to prolong rail life and improve railroad efficiency, rail grinders are designed to shave as little metal off the rail as possible. The amount of metal removed is measured in 100ths or 1000ths of an inch. In order to ensure that the proper amount of metal is removed, the grinding motor speed is carefully regulated. The working speed of the grinding train also has to be closely regulated and may be adjusted by tenths of a mile per hour. Although the grinders are capable of fairly high travel speeds, they move at just 1.5 to 15 miles per hour when working.

Rail grinding philosophy has evolved in the last few decades to reflect the changing needs of modern railroads and to take advantage of new technologies. New maintenance considerations have been developed to deal with increased train weights, higher tonnage, new types of rail alloys, and the introduction of three-phase alternating current locomotives with extremely high tractive effort and more effective dynamic braking capabilities. In the last decade, railroads have moved away from traditional corrective rail grinding practices and implemented progressive preventive strategies. Corrective rail grinding was aimed at repairing existing rail defects and was usually performed on a routine calendar basis. The rail grinding profiles were typically established by local railroad staff in charge of the line. By contrast, preventative rail grinding aims at keeping rail defects from occurring, while adjusting rail contours to achieve maximum locomotive performance and minimal wear. This type of maintenance does not depend on conventional visual rail inspections, but is based on the amount of tonnage over a section of line.

New grinding techniques have not been accepted by the entire industry. Some railroads have resisted adopting preventative rail grinding practices, partly because of the high cost of rail grinding. In 1993, the Advanced Rail Grinding Management Corporation estimated that rail grinding operations cost between $15,000 and $30,000 per day. Railroads must carefully weigh cost savings obtained through better rail profiling against the cost of performing preventative maintenance.

Types of Rail Grinders

Rail grinding, like rail defect detection, has long been a service contract to railroads. Traditionally, large production grinders, along with their specialized crew, would be hired by a railroad

A Speno rail grinder rolls through Waukesha on the Wisconsin Central's Chicago to Fond du Lac mainline. One of the most recognized names in rail grinding, Speno had special locomotives built by Electro-Motive Division. The RMS-1 rail grinding train used the Optical Rail Wear Inspection System to analyze track conditions.

to grind a section of mainline. The large production grinding trains are largely self-sufficient machines that carry all the supplies they need to work for days at a time. In recent years, smaller grinding trains have been developed. These are fully capable grinders, but designed for smaller-scale jobs and not necessarily intended for the same type of extended mainline grinding work that the larger trains do. In some situations, railways may purchase these smaller grinder trains rather than contract their services. The smaller grinding trains are often used on rapid-transit lines, where it would be impractical to hire a contract service because of clearance restrictions and other physical limitations.

Speno

Speno was a traditional name in rail grinding. Speno provided a contract rail grinding service to American railroads, and Speno rail grinding trains were a familiar sight all across the United States. One distinctive feature of Speno grinders was

that the grinding crew lived on board the trains in a bunk car as they traveled around. The company was based in East Syracuse, New York, along the former New York Central mainline between New York and Buffalo. Speno later became part of the Michigan-based Pandrol-Jackson, which subsequently became a component of Harsco Track Technologies. While the Speno name no longer appears on American grinding trains, the company left its mark, literally and figuratively, on the railroads.

The evolution of modern rail grinders is tied to advances in computer and visual recording technology, and to changes in railway maintenance philosophies. In the early 1980s, Speno developed a modern rail grinding train called the RMS-1 (RMS stands for Rail Maintenance System). This train was one of the first to use new electronic optical sensing technology as part of its pregrinding inspection. The RMS-1's Optical Rail Wear Inspection System provided detailed information on the rail profile that allowed for

immediate corrective action by the grinding heads. The recording equipment was designed to operate anywhere from 2 to 60 miles per hour, which gave Speno the flexibility to use the system during grinding operations or strictly as an inspection tool while the train traveled at full speed. The Optical Rail Wear Inspection System employed a high-speed video imaging system with a high-intensity flash to project light beams across the railhead, which were recorded by a special projector. This created a complete image of the rail profile for analysis. The video system was situated just 3 to 4 inches above the railhead, close enough to gather detailed, accurate information, but high enough to avoid the normal obstructions that are part of the track structure. As the RMS-1 worked, four different rail images—each one the product of a different camera—were monitored to assist with the operation. The output was recorded both on magnetic tape and as a printout. The grinder was designed for "fail-safe" grinding, to prevent overgrinding at very slow speeds. If the train suddenly slowed to speeds below the desired grinding speed, the grinding heads automatically retracted and the grinding stopped. Overgrinding removes more of the rails than is desired and can be counterproductive, as overgrinding may shorten rail life rather than lengthen it.

The RMS-1 was powered by two Electro-Motive Division (EMD) locomotives specially built for Speno. They incorporated basic components from two different standard EMD designs, the F40PH and GP38-2. The Speno locomotive carbodies were similar to those used for the F40PH, EMD's standard 3,000-horsepower passenger locomotive introduced in 1976; they are 56 feet, 2 inches long. Speno made some external modifications to the locomotive cab by extending the front windows forward to a point almost even with the plane of the locomotive nose. Unlike the F40PH, which was powered by a turbocharged 16-cylinder 645E engine that generated 3,000 horsepower for traction, Speno's locomotives had the power plant and other components normally used in EMD's popular GP38-2 road switcher. This included a normally aspirated 16-cylinder 645E engine that generated just 2,000 horsepower, and standard GP38-2 fuel tanks. Though EMD considered these locomotives variations of the

Opposite top and botttom
Speno bought secondhand GP38s from Conrail and remanufactured them with home-styled car bodies at its East Syracuse shops. When Pandrol-Jackson inherited Speno's rail grinding trains, it improved the locomotives' design and treated them to a blue-and-yellow paint job. *John Eagan*

GP38-2, they are usually classified as F40PH-2Ms. Between 1982 and 1985, EMD built a total of four of these locomotives for Speno. Some rail grinding trains were powered by former Conrail GP38-2s, which Speno rebuilt and shrouded with sheet metal at its shops. These peculiar, boxy locomotives are some of the strangest-looking machines on American rails. Speno's rail grinding locomotives carried the train's RMS designation in the number boards, with the locomotive number painted on the side of the engine.

In 1986, Speno outfitted an even more sophisticated, high-speed production grinding train, designated RMS-2. It was 625 feet long, comprising 12 cars. Like the RMS-1, it used a computer system to assist in profiling and grinding the rails. The onboard computer had up to 99 preprogrammed rail contour patterns stored in memory, and it was designed for higher productivity and greater flexibility than earlier machines. Precision automatic sensors and detailed rail contour patterns such as those employed on the RMS-2 allow a grinder to shave a minimum amount of steel off the rail. Thus, a modern computer-controlled grinder is a far more accurate and more efficient machine than those with a traditional design. Compared to the RMS-1, the RMS-2 also had easier-to-use computer software applications, which made running easier for the operators. The train was equipped with 120 rail grinding heads, each of which was powered by a 20-horsepower electric motor. The heads were paired in a way to avoid creating long wave form corrugations. As in other grinders, the stones were attached to a chuck on the motor to allow for rapid replacement. The RMS-2 was a bidirectional machine, arranged with a symmetrical consist with locomotives at each end.

Among other improvements over the RMS-1, the RMS-2 had more space on board for crew comfort and storage space for maintenance materials. New crew cars were designed to keep the crew from being disturbed by the grinding going on outside. Like other Speno trains, the RMS-2 was self-contained, allowing it to work for extended periods without having to interrupt work to secure supplies. This feature is particularly important when grinding on remote sections of track, such as in the American West and in Canada, where some railroad lines run through hundreds of miles of wilderness and sparsely settled territory. The train carried 14,000 gallons of fuel on board, which allowed it to run great distances between fuel stops. More importantly, it carried 44,000 gallons of water to prevent wildfires. Grinding continually produces hot sparks, and while efforts are made to contain the sparks, many escape the confines of the machine. Having

Loram's sophisticated rail grinder works BNSF's former Colorado & Southern line at Trinchera, Colorado. Burlington Northern Santa Fe has a progressive approach toward rail grinding, working with a preventative plan rather than the traditional corrective approach. A modern grinder such as this one is designed to reprofile rail with a single pass. *Howard Ande*

lots of water on board is imperative to keep the fire hazard at a minimum.

Speno's RMS-2 carried a nine-member company crew, including a supervisor, a foreman, two locomotive engineers, an electronics technician, a cook, and three support staffers to assist with general work. Rail grinding is no picnic and requires long working hours by the crew. When the train was out on the road, the crew might be with the train for months at a time, living and working in the same fashion as a Sperry rail detector crew.

Pandrol-Jackson

Pandrol-Jackson assumed grinding operations from Speno in the 1990s and continued to operate the same large grinding trains that Speno had developed, in addition to its own smaller grinding machines. Where Speno's trains were painted a safety orange and yellow, Pandrol-Jackson used a handsome dark blue-and-yellow scheme for its grinders (though for a time Pandrol's trains wore the old Speno colors with Pandrol-Jackson lettering). Pandrol-Jackson introduced its RMS-5 grinder in 1997, which used many of the fundamental components of earlier Speno grinders, including the same rebuilt GP38 and F40PH-2M locomotives. In addition to the two locomotives, the RMS-5 grinder was composed of nine cars, arranged in the following order: two crew cars, three grinding cars, two water and fuel storage cars, and two generator cars. The three grinding cars carried a total of 96 motorized grinding heads, 48 on each side of the train. Each of these grinding heads was powered by a 30-horsepower electric motor, and they were angled in place by a hydraulic control. A grinding command center was situated on the second grinding car. The dorm and kitchen cars for the crew had been converted from former GO Transit commuter rail cars from Toronto. The generator cars, which generated electricity for the grinders, were equipped with a 16-cylinder Caterpillar diesel engine. The RMS-5 was designed to grind about 80 miles of track a day, but it had been known to accomplish 20 percent more than that on very productive days. It used a specially built speed regulator called a Pace Setter, manufactured by an outside vendor, to maintain precise speed control when the train was grinding at very slow

speeds. One of the locomotives also powered a dust collection system to minimize environmental damage from the grinding.

Harsco Track Technologies

Harsco Track Technologies produces several varieties of commercial rail grinding machines that incorporate the latest advances in rail grinding technology. The PGM-48 (which stands for Production Grinder, Magnum) mainline grinder is a self-propelled, self-contained machine designed to produce optimum-profile rails and remove defects, such as corrugations and rail lips.

It uses a modern computer network to control and monitor all its grinding functions and the speed of the machine. This technology allows a single human operator to oversee the rail grinding procedures. As suggested by its designation, the PGM-48 has a total of 48 grinder heads, 24 on each side of the train, which are carried by three grinding cars. They use standard 10-inch grinding stones. The grinding heads are powered by 30-horsepower motors that turn at speeds up to 3,600 rpm. Two Cummins KTA38 diesel engines power the train. The PGM-48 is double ended and fully capable of grinding in either direction at a maximum speed of 15 miles per hour (24 kilometer per hour). When it isn't grinding, the train can travel at a top speed of 50 miles per hour, and can be towed in consist at even faster speeds. Compared to the older Speno and Pandrol-Jackson grinders, the PGM-48 is relatively short, measuring only 208 feet (63.43 meters) long. It is 15 feet, 2 inches (4.629 meters) tall.

Harsco's PGM-48 grinder is a Cadillac compared to the dirty, dusty, old-fashioned grinding trains of days past. Crews work in pressurized, soundproof, climate-controlled cabins that feature comfortable padded seats. They are designed to

Two venerable Southern Pacific SD9s lead a water train at Long Ravine, California, in July 1990. The train is making a dash up grade to Cape Horn to extinguish a brushfire started by a rail grinder.

provide the operators with easy access to the controls, while maintaining a clear view of the tracks. Harsco also manufactures smaller versions of the Magnum series grinder in configurations of either 16 or 32 grinding motors.

Harsco's Production Transit Grinder is a smaller machine designed for lighter jobs. It is a flexible unit intended for both mainline and switch grinding. It can be configured with 8 to 32 grinding heads. Like the Magnum series, the Production Transit Grinder has sophisticated modern computer controls and rail recording systems. Among its other features are a track vacuum that sucks up particulates left over from the grinding process, a dust collection system that sucks up airborne particulates (see the RGHC/TVC-A1 system described later), and an obstruction avoidance system.

Harsco's Model RGHC is a small self-propelled grinder designed for both domestic and international applications. Although sometimes overshadowed by the larger production grinding trains, the RGHC is a fully capable modern grinder. It is suitable for grinding rails in accordance with many different corrective or preventative profiles. It comes in 8- and 10-stone units, which may be operated singly or in multiple, depending on the nature of the grinding required. This machine is designed to eliminate and prevent several common types of rail defects, including long waves, track vibration corrugations, and millscale.

The RGHC grinder is extremely compact compared to the massive multi-unit grinders. It measures just 37 feet, 9 inches long; 8 feet, 4 inches wide; and a little more than 12 feet tall—smaller than the average boxcar traditionally found on North American railroads. The eight-unit machine weighs 69,500 pounds. The grinder is propelled by a diesel engine with a hydrostatic transmission system and is capable of a travel speed of 62 miles per hour. (Why 62 miles per hour? This train is designed for overseas applications where metric measurements are standard, so while 62 miles per hour seems like an odd top speed, it converts neatly to the metric equivalent of 100 kilometers per hour.) The grinders are available in fixed standard gauge versions (4 feet, 8.5 inches) as well variable gauge versions that can be used on track as narrow as 3 feet, 6 inches (1,067 millimeters), which is a standard gauge in many countries of the world, including Japan. The grinding motors are hydraulically powered and work at a maximum of 20 horsepower, rotating at between 5,500 and 6,000 rpm. The grinder works at speeds between 2 and 11 miles per hour, depending on the grinding required. Like other grinders, the machine is speed sensitive, automatically adjusting the speed of the motors to compensate for changes in forward velocity, and thus preventing overgrinding of the rails. It can grind track as steep as 6 percent, which is about twice as steep as any American mainline.

The grinding motors are located between the driving wheels, below the body of the machine. They are carefully centered over the rails, with four grinders per rail. The grinding heads are mounted independently of one another, allowing for precise adjustment of each grinding stone, as dictated by the chosen rail profile. The onboard computer can be programmed with nearly 100 different grinding patterns. The heads are retractable, so they can be lifted out of the way if there is an obstruction that interferes with grinding or threatens to damage the equipment. This grinder is specially designed to grind difficult track sections that other grinders might not be able to handle well, such as switches, crossings, and highway level crossings. The rapidly spinning stones are guarded by fire-resistant spark shields and other equipment specifically designed to keep dangerous sparks from potentially igniting fires along the tracks. Heat sensors are also included to warn crew members of excessive heat, alerting them should a fire start during grinding. When the machine is in operation, water nozzles douse the tracks with a water mist to keep dust down and minimize the fire risks. In addition, the grinder has a chemical fire-extinguishing system and high-pressure hoses with adjustable nozzles for putting out wildfires.

Modern grinders such as the RGHC have much nicer crew cabins than old fashioned grinders, and compared to the old machines, the control room on today's machine seems space-aged. It is pressurized and insulated to minimize the effects of vibration, noise, and dust, which can be quite severe on a grinder, yet the cabin has large windows that give operators a fine view of the tracks. The windows are made from argon-filled double-paned glass.

Grinding functions on the RGHC are controlled by an onboard computer. This computer has to be extremely durable in order to endure the difficult and potentially damaging conditions imposed by the harsh grinding environment. Operators direct the grinding on a touchscreen monitor, and the computer has built-in diagnostic functions to assist operators in event of a failure or other problems. Since this type of grinder is designed for foreign sales, the computer is flexible and can be programmed for use in different languages, making machine operation easier for non-English speakers.

The RGHC grinders can be arranged in a three-car configuration that consists of two eight-stone grinders bracketing a TVC-A1 track vacuum. This machine creates negative air pressure below the grinders to suck up dust and grinding debris. The ability to control dust and sparks is one of the most important attributes of modern grinders outside of their rail profiling functions.

Loram

Loram has been in the rail grinding business for decades. Its mustard yellow articulated rail grinders are a familiar sight on railroad lines. Loram's grinding trains are not as complicated nor as long as the old Speno trains, in part because the Loram crews do not live on board the trains. Instead they are housed off-site when they are not working. Loram prides itself on its high level of crew training, which is more extensive than that required to meet railroad safety procedures. Since rail grinders have a propensity to start wildfires, Loram provides its crews with training in firefighting. Its older grinding trains carried a specially equipped caboose with firefighting equipment for quickly extinguishing fires ignited by stray sparks. Like its older trains, Loram's modern rail grinder is equipped with a fire prevention and protection system.

Loram recently introduced a modern, sophisticated grinding unit that employs up-to-date sensing and computer-regulated grinding technology. Through exhaustive research, Loram developed a rail grinding machine that uses highly effective computerized rail profile selection, modern grinding stones, and metal removal. Loram's rail analysis system, which is known by the acronym VISTA for *VIS*ion *T*ransverse *A*nalyzer, uses optical technology to assess rail surface conditions for comparison with remedial surfacing profiles in preparation for grinding. Loram boasts that its modern grinders are available to work 98 percent of the time, and its crews often work as many as 300 shifts a year. Loram grinders operate all over North America and in several countries around the world.

A Day With the Grinder

A typical grinding crew reports for work at 6 A.M. and expects to put in a full day. In the summer, a grinder sometimes will work at night to take advantage of the cooler temperatures and naturally forming dew to help minimize the risk of fire. A grinder may also work at night to avoid interfering with train schedules, since some lines, particularly those with heavy suburban passenger traffic, operate most of their trains in normal daytime hours. Typically, when a grinder is assigned to a line it may work six days a week, allowing the seventh for rest and maintenance. Representatives of the railroad ride on board when the grinder is working, including an official, such as a track superintendent.

Before grinding begins, a plan of action is worked out with the railroad. Rail profiles need to be selected in advance, and the amount of time the grinder will have to work on each section of track is decided. Some profiles can be achieved relatively quickly, with just one pass of the machine, while others require more attention and slower grinding. Deciding which grinding patterns to use can be quite a complicated business, and this is one area where the use of sophisticated computers helps considerably.

Winter is one of the best times to grind rail, since the risk from brushfires caused by sparks is much lower. On February 1, 2000, a Pandrol-Jackson rail grinding train rolls through Mechanicville, New York.
Jim Shaughnessy

Loram's rail grinder No. 6 works at twilight along Southern Pacific's Dalsa Cutoff at Caldwell, Texas, on March 29, 1992. This train, outfitted in 1981, has 88 grinders. It was one of more than a dozen Loram grinders in operation at that time.
Tom Kline

Water Trains

The fire protection train is one of the more unusual specialty maintenance trains. These trains date back to 1870, when they were needed to keep the many miles of wooden snowsheds on California's Donner Pass from conflagration. The combination of wooden sheds, sparks from locomotives, and unusually dry air made for a high fire risk much of the year in the Sierra. Shortly after the opening of the transcontinental route, fire trains were deemed a necessity to keep the line open and safe. While Donner Pass was known for its extraordinary winter weather, which required the snowsheds to begin with, the high, dry summer and autumn seasons also proved challenging to railroad operations. At one time, four fire trains were stationed at key points on the line between Roseville, California, and Sparks, Nevada. These could be found at Truckee, Summit station, Blue Cañon, and Colfax. Each train was kept on alert, ready to go at a moment's notice to fight fires.

The original fire trains consisted of rectangular tank cars hauled by 4-4-0s, including the famous *Governor Stanford*. The tanks held 7,200 gallons of water, which were delivered by pumps on the engines at a rate of 150 gallons per minute. By the 1890s, these trains were replaced by even better ones. They were hauled by 4-6-0s and featured more powerful pumps and headlights on the tenders to permit quick reversing at night. Central Pacific maintained several fire lookouts at key locations along its line to watch for fires. The stations were manned by a telegrapher who could alert the men on the railroad in the event of a blaze. In the days before telephones or radio, it was especially important to have a reliable communications system and a plan of action to deal with an emergency. In today's world of two-way radios, mobile phones, fax machines, and the Internet, it may be difficult to comprehend how isolated communities were in the nineteenth century. A fire could be raging out of control between Emigrant Gap and the Summit, and trains climbing eastward would be oblivious to the problem until they were practically upon it. Making matters even more serious, the railroad was covered by shed for more than 30 continuous miles at the highest elevations. Once a fire got going, it had the potential to be enormously destructive.

The heyday of the fire train was over by the 1920s. Donner Pass had been converted to double track, and the railroad was able to eliminate many of the snowsheds by using large Leslie rotary plows to keep the tracks clear (see chapter 7). The fire train did survive into the modern era, however, to protect the remaining sheds and to minimize the risk from brushfires. By the 1990s, a water train was called out only on rare occasions, usually accompanying a rail grinder to both dampen the ground ahead of the grinding and scamper back to extinguish any fires caused by the grinding sparks. The modern water train used specially assigned tank cars painted in maintenance-of-way gray and stenciled "water car." The cars were equipped with high-pressure pumps and towed by diesels, usually old GP9s or SD9s.

Workers on an SP water train spray down the tracks in advance of a rail grinder to prevent sparks from igniting wildfires along the tracks. The water train carries several hundred thousand gallons of water and high-pressure water cannons, as well as a caboose.

6

Speeders and Hyrails

The romantic appeal of the handcar has made it one of the most endearing types of railway maintenance equipment. The average Joe on the street wouldn't know a ballast regulator from a rotary plow, but he'd certainly recognize an old fashioned handcar. You know the kind; you've seen them in old movies and morning cartoons. The handcar is little more than a basic platform with a pivoting beam to drive the wheels and takes two people to operate see saw fashion. In these portrayals we often see two hapless characters propelling themselves along the tracks on such a contraption, without authorization or permission from a dispatcher or anyone else; they zip into a tunnel, we hear the "toot" of a steam whistle or the "honk" of a diesel horn, and we see them again, pumping as fast as they can to stay ahead of a speeding express train. While this portrayal of the device is flawed, such machines were once quite common on American railroads. They were used by section gangs to travel along the track and move equipment.

Though handcars were simple, inexpensive, and didn't require much maintenance, they were labor-intensive to operate, limiting their usefulness. A variation of the handcar was the bicycle-like three-wheel velocipede. Also reliant on human power to make it go, the velocipede was compara-

The Canadian firm of Woodings manufactured speeders in competition with Fairmont. Although relatively rare today, a few Woodings are still puttering about. On October 2, 1997, a New Brunswick Southern crew inspects the former Canadian Pacific mainline at Matawaumkeg, Maine.

The traditional handcar is a classic icon of railroading. In this photograph by William Bullard from circa 1905, a section gang poses with its Fairbanks-Morse handcar on Boston & Albany's North Brookfield Branch. These cars were eventually displaced by motorized speeders. *William Bullard, courtesy of Dennis LeBeau*

Right
A Fairmont MT-19 speeder rides through pine forests on the Moscow, Camden & San Augustine. The most basic in rail transportation, Fairmont speeders were the vehicle of choice for track inspectors and maintenance crews for many years, though they are now relatively scarce. *Tom Kline*

tively lightweight. A renegade Michigan inventor named George S. Sheffield is credited with selling the first railroad velocipedes. As the story goes, in the late 1870s, Sheffield experimented with velocipede designs on the nearby Michigan Central. He did this without the railroad's consent and eventually ran into difficulties with the company, which was displeased with the unauthorized use of its tracks. Despite these hurdles, Sheffield's experimentation eventually led him to form the Sheffield Velocipede Company, which supplied rail velocipedes to the railroad industry. In 1893, the company made a technological leap and patented a two-cycle gasoline engine, which led to the development of a whole line of gasoline-powered rail motor cars. These early designs sparked a whole generation of motor cars produced by several different companies.

Fairbanks-Morse

Around the turn of the nineteenth century, the railroad equipment manufacturer Fairbanks-Morse acquired the Sheffield company and inte-

grated its two lines of track cars. (Fairbanks-Morse is probably best remembered today for its foray into building diesel-electric locomotives in the 1940s and 1950s.) In the early part of the twentieth century, motorized track cars were listed in the Fairbanks-Morse catalog along with handcars and velocipedes, and the company pictured motorized track cars in its 1908 catalog. One advertisement read, "Gasoline Motor Car, send for spe-

cial descriptive circular," and went on to list "hand and push cars, velocipedes, tracklaying cars, gasoline engines, gasoline turntable motors," among other items. Another entry depicts a slightly more detailed image of a motorized track car, with all the luxury of a tiny engine and three padded seat cushions for the comfort of the crew. The text below the entry described the features of this gaspowered motor car:

No. 2 Fairbanks-Morse Gasoline Motor Car, direct-connected. For three persons. This car is identical with our No. 1 car, excepting as follows: tool box is placed under front seat, also has extra guide arm and wheel for greater stiffness in running. All machinery parts interchangeable with No. 1 car. Weight, ready for service, 385 lbs.; packed for export, 700 lbs.

Fairmont's MT motor cars were lightweight machines. Most MT models were equipped with air-cooled, two-cylinder, four-cycle Onan engines. Here Don Neale and Andrew Hudanish turn a Fairmont MT-4 motor car on the tracks at Moscow, Texas, on August 5, 2000. *Tom Kline*

The entry further explained that both the No. 1 and No. 2 motor cars were normally equipped with a "mechanical sparking device," or what we now call a sparkplug. These basic Fairbanks-Morse motor cars were primitive machines, as stingy with amenities as F-M's ad copy was with articles and verbs!

The velocipedes and handcars offered in the same Fairbanks-Morse catalog were equally Spartan. The "No. 1 Velocipede Car" was little more than three thin-spoked flanged wheels, a pumping handle for propulsion, and a hard-backed seat. The car weighed just 150 pounds, but it was equipped with ball bearings! The "No. 2 Velocipede Car" shared most of the same qualities as the No. 1 car, except it had the addition of an auxiliary seat to carry a passenger and the ultimate luxury of a footrest for the driver. F-M was quite pleased with this model and exclaimed in the description, "It makes an excellent inspection car, as the inspector can sit facing the track and carefully note its condition as the car proceeds." All these extra amenities on the No. 2 model weighed an additional 5 pounds.

F-M's handcars with the famous two-person walking-beam propulsion system were a bit more substantial than the velocipedes. There was the "No. 20 Standard Section Hand Car," which weighed 555 pounds and had 3-inch-high side rails on the deck, presumably to keep tools from bouncing off as the car zipped along. The real

queen of the rails, the big handcar, was the "No. 2 Special Hand Car." Though short in the comfort department, it had lots of selling points superior to other models. Its platform was 7 feet, 6 inches long by 4 feet, 4.25 inches wide. As might be surmised by its narrow width, the wheels bracketed the outside of the frame. Narrow, frame benches were located on each side to serve as seats for passengers—the passengers being railroad crewmen on their way to a job site, not the paying kind found in the coaches and Pullman cars of a railroad's fancy express trains. The standard wheels were made from 20-inch pressed steel, although a customer could order wood center wheels as an option. The walking beam was slightly longer on this car, making it easier to propel the car. The longer beam was certainly needed, because the car itself weighed 650 pounds and could carry about six passengers in addition to the pumping crewmen.

Looking back at the motorized cars in Fairbanks-Morse's catalog, one model stands out above the rest: the "No. 16, Type 'C' Fairbanks-Morse Inspection Motor Car." Not only is the car much nicer, but its description is slightly more literate: "This car is designed especially for inspection work; it has three seats crosswise, two facing forward and one backward. This car seats nine people and the maximum speed is about 35 miles [per hour]." This machine actually had an overhead covering, a windscreen, and a "cow catcher" in case of "incident."

Fairmont Motor Cars

Among the best-known manufacturers of rail motors cars was the Fairmont Gas Engine and Railway Motor Car Company of Fairmont, Minnesota. Between 1911 and 1991, Fairmont produced an estimated 73,000 motor cars for use in North America and around the world. It had more than 18 different car models constructed for use on a variety of track widths, ranging from 2-foot gauge to 5-foot, 6-inch gauge. For much of the twentieth century, the Fairmont motor car, in one shape or another, was a standard fixture on most American railways.

Early Fairmont motor cars used a small one-cylinder, two-cycle engine for propulsion. This simple internal combustion engine sounds much like that used on a lawn mower, making a "putt-putt-putt" sound. Unlike most heavy motorized cars in use today, many of the first cars did not have an adjustable transmission system to modulate the power of the engine, and instead used a direct drive, whereby the engine was permanently coupled to the drive axle. As a result, the machine had to be in motion when the engine was running; if it stopped, the engine stalled. To get the engine

Motor cars offer railroads a cheap, simple vehicle for maintenance crews. Members of a Maine Central section gang stow equipment at Cumberland Mills on the fabled Mountain Subdivision in October 1982. The daily freight from South Portland's Rigby Yard to St. Johnsbury, Vermont, will be along in a few minutes, and the gang needs to get "in the clear." *Brian Jennison*

running again, the car had to be pushed along the tracks. To reverse the engine, a minor adjustment was made to the sparkplug (yes, just one plug for the one cylinder), and the engine was started in the opposite direction. A simple coil was used to produce the electrical charge needed to fire the sparkplug. Eventually a drive belt transmission was introduced, which offered a level of power output control. The drive belt typically was made from a heavy-duty industrial fabric. While a fabric might seem a tenuous choice for power transmission, a properly maintained belt could last up to 40,000 miles in regular service.

By the 1950s, Fairmont was building cars with more advanced engine and transmission designs. Some cars came equipped with modern, powerful, two-cylinder, four-stroke engines, and featured mechanical transmission drive operated

with a clutch. These more advanced motor cars had many advantages over the early models, but some railroads preferred the simplicity and low cost of the older two-cycle engine models, so Fairmont kept the older designs in production.

As with the early Fairbanks-Morse cars, the typical Fairmont cars had few frills and generally offered the most basic mechanized rail transportation possible. The simplest Fairmont motor car was little more than a motor, four wheels, and a simple platform. Accessories were available to improve the condition of different railcar models, and they varied from model to model. Some cars were very small, designed to carry just two people, while others were relatively large to carry six or more riders.

The typical Fairmont was capable of speeds of 20 to 40 miles per hour on level track. Today, 40

Dating back to the 1950s, Hyrail vehicles have largely superseded the traditional motor car or speeder. On July 24, 1958, a Ford Hyrailer rolls along the Illinois Central at Centralia, Illinois. *Richard Jay Solomon*

miles per hour might not seem very fast, but when you are bouncing along on the hard seat of a motor car with neither seat belt nor any other protection between you and the great outdoors, and with the ties passing by—zip, zip, zip—just inches from your feet, even a mere 35 miles per hour seems like light speed. The cars were generally equipped with a fairly basic braking system, consisting of cast-iron brake shoes that were pressed against the wheels.

Fairmont's M-9 was one of its most basic models. It was an older style belt-driven car, intended as a two-passenger inspection car. It could be ordered with either a one- or two-cylinder, two-cycle engine, which powered the rear axle. Like an old lawn mower, the engine was the traditional pull-start variety. The car had a very short wheelbase, and as a stock car, the M-9 did not come with a windshield, roof, outside protective covering, or even proper seat cushions. All these features could be purchased as extras at the discretion of the railroad. A slightly larger, heavier car was the M-14, which lacked a suspension system and other amenities. The M-19 was a four-person model, slightly lighter than the M-14, and equipped with suspension.

Fairmont's MT model cars were similar to the M models, but most were equipped with a two-cylinder, four-cycle Onan engine that was air-cooled, rather than water-cooled. This engine used an opposed piston design—the pistons faced one another in a common cylinder—which produced between 18 and 22 horsepower. Perhaps the most important difference in the MT models, and the reason for the "T" in the designation, was their two-speed design. Most of these cars had a mechanical two-speed transmission operated with a dry clutch. The MT series cars could be equipped with enclosed aluminum cabs, heaters, and comfortable cushioned seats. With such lavish luxuries afforded on motor car crews, it must have baffled cynical railroad managers how such pampered men could get any real work done at all!

Among the later Fairmont designs were the Model A motor cars, which came in various sizes and were equipped with larger engines than most motor cars. The A-8 model was the biggest of the bunch, powered with a six-cylinder engine, often a Ford 300-ci. Unlike most Fairmont motor cars, the A-8 had a long wheelbase and a solid suspension system that used both springs and shock absorbers to provide a comfortable ride.

Woodings

Woodings was another common brand of motor car, and a few are still in use. These cars were manufactured in Canada and favored by Canadian lines. Woodings cars were normally enclosed and built with a suspension system. They were equipped with a mechanical transmission similar to that used in snowmobiles. Woodings cars were powered by a single-cylinder, four-stroke engine that produced between 16 and 18 horsepower.

The Demise of the Motor Car

The use of traditional railcars for track maintenance and inspection greatly diminished over the years. Fifty years ago, motor cars were a common sight on all American railroads. They can still be found in regular use today, but motor cars are becoming increasingly rare. The motor car was advantageous for several reasons. It was a comparatively cheap and simple machine that was easy to maintain and operate. It was lightweight and so could be loaded on and off the tracks quickly and easily, and it was easily stowed away. Railroads maintained railcar storage sheds along the right-of-way that faced the mainline, with stub-end tracks and groups of ties between the rails to facilitate the loading and unloading of railcars. Most railcars had retractable wooden handles designed to pull the cars onto the tracks. Railcars were ideal for the rapid deployment of work crews and light equipment along the line, particularly in areas that were not easily accessed by highways. Since railcars ran close to the ground, they allowed inspectors a good look at the tracks. The lack of suspension and passenger comforts in the cars probably actually facilitated inspection and repair of tough track. If a track inspector felt a big bump as he motored along, it was a pretty good sign that the track needed attention.

The decline of the motor car speeder can be attributed to a number of factors. Since the end of World War II, American railroads have changed the ways they go about carrying out their track maintenance. The day of the traditional section gang is gone. Instead of localized gangs assigned to a specific section of track, railroads use roving gangs that specialize in a particular facet of maintenance. Since specialized gangs have to travel greater distances, they have less need for speeders, and are often moved in buses, trucks, and work trains. With the introduction of modern maintenance machines and a smaller railroad network, far fewer people are required to maintain track. Prior to the advent of motorized cars and trucks and the development of a paved highway system, railroad maintenance

Although largely superseded by modern Hyrail trucks, the traditional motorized speeder still has a place on some railroads. A Southern Pacific Fairmont speeder and trailer are seen at Truckee, California. Snow removal crews use speeders to carry equipment to difficult-to-reach places.

was rail based; in other words, maintenance crews relied on the railroad to maintain it. In most cases, this is no longer true. Highway access has been dramatically improved over the years, and today most railroad locations can be reached by rubber-tired vehicles on access roads. The conversion of many lines from double to single track facilitated the building of maintenance roads along the right-of-way. On the former New York Central Railroad and Pennsylvania Railroad mainlines, only two tracks remain where there once were four or more, providing ample space for a broad, well-surfaced access road along much of the routes.

The development of Hyrail technology (described later in the chapter) also played a large role in the disappearance of traditional motor cars. Using Hyrail wheel sets, most common cars and trucks can be fitted to operate on railroad tracks. Hyrail vehicles have a number of advantages over motor cars. They can get on and off tracks easily at most highway crossings, and they can travel on the road as easily as on the rails, making them much more flexible than motor cars. This flexibility makes them better suited to modern maintenance practices. A Hyrail truck also has all the comforts of a modern vehicle—proper suspension, ergonomic padded seats, heat and air conditioning, windshield wipers—little things that tend to make them a lot more agreeable to crews than the

A Fairmont speeder at Belfast & Moosehead Lake's yards in Belfast, Maine. Speeders survive on many shortline railroads and are popular with hobbyists. *Stephen D. Carlson*

bouncy, open-air motor cars. In many situations where speeders might be called for, Hyrail trucks are used instead.

Speeder Holdouts and Speeder Hobbyists

Virtually no new speeders have been built for American railroads in the last decade, and most railroads have dispensed with speeder fleets in favor of Hyrail trucks and other transport methods. However, a few cars have been sold to lines overseas where more traditional maintenance methods still prevail, and even in this country, despite the major changes in the maintenance climate, the motor car speeder has not yet become totally extinct. Speeders have held on in few places, such as on remote sections of track, where highway access is severely restricted and where it may be difficult for Hyrail vehicles to get out of the way of trains. The two primary Sierra crossings in California have used speeder-based maintenance for this reason. Both the former Southern Pacific line over Donner Pass and the former Western Pacific route through the Feather River Canyon enjoy the colorful practice of speeder-car operation many years after other lines gave up on them. Likewise, Canadian Pacific lines serving remote areas favored speeders because of difficult access.

Although the number of active speeders has dramatically declined in the last few decades, they are one of the few types of railway maintenance equipment that have attracted serious interest from railroad hobbyists and preservation groups. Thousands of the traditional speeder cars are now privately owned. The romance of riding the rails in an open or semiopen car has great appeal to

hobbyists. It's like sleeping in the outdoors: when one is forced to do it, we call it "survival"; when one chooses to do it, we call it "camping." The first is because one has no other choice, while the other is for pleasure. The simplicity of the speeders, combined with the quirky technology and the historical and romantic connotations, have great appeal in the modern world. In this way the speeder has come full circle. It was developed by an amateur for the pleasure of riding the rails, and in its retirement, it has again become the tool of amateur rail riders.

This is not to say that speeder owners can just set down their historic Fairmonts or Woodings on the nearest set of tracks and speed away. This may sound like a tempting adventure to the novice enthusiast, but such activity would be more dangerous than skateboarding on the interstate at night—blindfolded! Speeder trips, whether initiated by the railroad for maintenance purposes or by enthusiasts wishing to travel over a stretch of tracks, must be approved by the railroad that owns and operates the tracks and coordinated with a dispatcher. Even a trip over very lightly used line must be properly coordinated to prevent accidents.

Amateur speeder owners typically belong to an organization that arranges motor car trips over different railway lines, and ensures a level of safety among members through strict operating rules. The largest of these motor groups is the North American Railcar Operators Association (NARCO). Motor car excursions can involve dozens of speeders, and proper coordination of such events is essential. Excursions are scheduled in advance with the owning railroad, and usually the railroad will send a Hyrail truck with an official to pilot the excursionists over the line. Some excursions are relatively short trips, others traverse hundreds of miles and can last for days.

Hyrail Trucks

The Hyrail truck does now what the motor car once did. It is basically just a normal over-the-road type of truck that has been equipped with pilot wheels to guide it along the tracks. While the modern Hyrail vehicle has become popular only in the last few decades, rail-equipped automobiles have been around since the early days of the private car. These early automobiles on steel wheels generally served as inspection vehicles. Unlike the modern Hyrail truck, they did not have the flexibility to get on and off the rails easily.

The Hyrail's function and ability has moved well beyond the basic pickup truck on the rails. Today, Hyrail technology has permitted a large variety of different vehicles to be equipped with adjustable steel wheels for operation both on the rails and on the highway. Boom trucks, welding trucks, payloaders, and cranes are all now routinely fitted with some variety of Hyrail wheels.

The type of Hyrail wheels employed largely depends on the size of the vehicle and the weight of its intended load. Hyrail wheel attachments have several basic requirements. They are, of course, flanged to keep the vehicle on the tracks, yet they need to be fully retractable so they do not interfere with the vehicle while driving on the highway. The wheels need to provide sufficient support for the vehicle when operating on the tracks, but they should not weigh more than necessary, since additional weight reduces fuel efficiency and limits the vehicle's load-hauling capacity. When a vehicle is running on the rails with Hyrail wheels, it is still propelled by its conventional rubber tires. A suspension system is necessary to avoid rough riding on the rails, while at the same time maintaining adequate adhesion for

Modern railroads use Hyrail trucks for a great many purposes. A Burlington Northern Hyrail driver gives a friendly wave on a clear September 1989 morning at Mendota, Illinois.

One of the advantages of a Hyrail truck is that it can be easily set on and off the tracks at level highway crossings. Earle Leeson manually lowers the flanged guide wheels on a Hyrail truck at Harwood, Texas, on December 9, 2000. *Tom Kline*

Hyrailing along the Texas, Gonzales & Northern mainline at speed. The beauty of a Hyrail truck is that it uses its rubber-tired wheels for propulsion while metal guide wheels keep the vehicle on track. The steering column is locked in place to preclude any difficulties.
Tom Kline

propulsion. A steering wheel lock is provided to keep the wheels straight when in rail mode. Lastly, Hyrail wheels must easily deploy and retract to allow the vehicle to get on and off the tracks quickly and easily.

Hyrail wheels for small trucks can be made from aluminum or steel, and a mechanical system may be used to raise and lower the guide wheels. For example, Harsco's HR0307 Series A HY-RAIL guide wheels, designed for trucks with a load capacity of 700 pounds, use aluminum wheels and frames. The front and rear wheel sets weigh 255 pounds each, not including the nominal weight of the mounting equipment. The wheels themselves are set 4 feet, 8.5 inches apart (the standard American track gauge), and they are just 10 inches in diameter, with a flange diameter of 12.25 inches; they are much smaller than conventional wheels on locomotive and freight car designs. The wheels may be ordered with either a steel or rubber tread. Since these wheel sets are relatively lightweight, they are applied using a simple mechanical system, called an Easy-Lift actuator.

For larger trucks running on the tracks, Harsco offers more substantial HY-RAIL packages. This means heavier equipment, more substantial wheels and suspension, and hydraulic controls to raise and lower the guide wheels. The use of a "support carriage" transfers the vehicle's load from the rubber tire wheels to the steel guiding wheels for better suspension.

For a Hyrail truck to get on the tracks, it must be properly positioned at a grade crossing. The truck should be turned to line up with the tracks in the direction of travel, and the guide wheels lowered and locked into place. The steering column must be locked, and then the truck is ready to proceed down the track. Most American mainlines are inspected daily by a track foreman or other official driving a Hyrail truck, and it is quite common to see a railroad pickup cruising along on the tracks. Usually the passing of a Hyrail truck means there isn't much rail traffic in the area, as a dispatcher will only give a Hyrail truck permission to occupy the tracks after all trains are out of the way.

Modern signaling and dispatching systems have taken a lot of the risk out of railroading, but mistakes and accidents still happen. The driver of a Hyrail truck has to be extremely careful. If trains and trucks attempt to occupy the same section of track at the same time, the Hyrail always loses. I recall two incidents involving Hyrail trucks that illustrate the seriousness of this point. The first took place on Conrail's former New York Central mainline near Batavia, New York, in the spring of 1989. There is a big curve at Batavia, and then the railroad straightens out for a nearly 30-mile run of tangent track to Buffalo. This line is under the authority of Centralized Traffic Control, which means that dispatcher-controlled signals authorize train movements, but Hyrail vehicles and other maintenance equipment had to be given verbal authority over the radio to occupy the tracks. On the day in question in 1989, a track-car driver on the mainline, making a routine trip west from the Rochester area, radioed into the Buffalo mainline dispatcher and asked for permission to occupy the No. 1 track between Batavia and a point near Corfu. This was, and still is, a normal procedure. The dispatcher responded, asking the driver where he wanted to go. The driver said he needed permission to use the track between CP (control point) 402 to mileage 410. The dispatcher agreed and gave him the authority he asked for, and then he asked, "Where are you now?"

"I'm at Milepost 400."

The dispatcher, suddenly sounding alarmed, replied, "Well, I just gave you the track from 402 to 410. Your previous authority

Tragedy at Bahia

expired at 400. How do you propose getting from 400 to 402?"

There was a shocked silence.

The dispatcher came on again, this time quite angry, "Listen, mister, that's how people get killed!"

After a bit, I assume, the track-car driver got where he was going, however humbled by his mistake. Not all track-car drivers are so lucky.

A few years later, fellow photographer and author Brian Jennison and I were photographing along Southern Pacific's "Cal-P" (California Pacific) mainline in the vicinity of Martinez, California. It was a thick foggy spring day, and we were looking for a suitable place to make a set of Amtrak No. 6, the eastbound *California Zephyr*. We considered going across the Carquinez Straits to a location known as Bahia, but decided against it on account of the fog. Instead, we set up for a shot on a bluff overlooking the straits near SP's Ozol Yard on the west side of Martinez. Amtrak No. 6 rolled passed, and we made our photographs. Then, about 10 minutes later, the engineer called the dispatcher over the train radio.

"This is No. 6. I'm in 'Emergency' [an emergency brake application]. We've just struck a Hyrail truck at Bahia. Call an ambulance!"

I learned later that the driver of the Hyrail died on the spot. A year or so after the incident I was back at the grade crossing at Bahia, and noticed that a wreath of flowers had been hung on the meter maid there. (A "meter maid" is a track-occupancy indicator, consisting of a small semaphore sealed behind glass.) I'll always wonder, if we had decided to take our pictures at Bahia, instead of Ozol, could we have warned the Hyrail driver?

As the sun sets over the American River Gorge, a track inspector takes a closer look at a potential defect at Old Gorge on the west slope of California's Donner Pass on December 15, 1989. While riding the rails in a Hyrail provides some spectacular views, these trucks have to share the tracks with larger and much heavier trains.

Snow Plows

On a weed-grown spur behind the shop, or at the far end of the yard, sits a railroad's oldest and least-used rolling stock. Their builder plates read 1907 or 1916 or 1920, and they are 20 years older than the newest steam locomotive the railroad owned—a locomotive that was cut up for scrap more than 40 years ago. What are these antiques doing on the property? Why haven't they been hauled off for scrap years ago? These are the snowplows, waiting for that big storm that shuts down the railroad, or waiting to clear that lightly used branch that has sat idly for weeks during the winter. On some lines a plow may wait out the whole winter without turning a wheel, while on others, a plow might see weekly or even daily service to clear the line.

Wedge Plows

Light snow can be easily cleared from the tracks by small pilot plows permanently fixed to the locomotives. But when an arctic storm or nor'easter blows through, and snow is measured in feet rather than inches, the railroad drags out its ancient plows and sends them out on the line. One of the most common styles of big railway snowplows was the "wedge plow." This descriptively named machine is exactly what it sounds like: a wedge-shaped plow. It is essentially a huge knife blade that is pushed along at speed, forcing accumulated snow off the tracks.

A typical type of wedge plow that is still in use is the Russell plow, built after World War I. This steel-framed machine features a Spartan wooden interior, an adjustable front

A Southern Pacific rotary plow clears snow from the eastbound tracks at Yuba Pass, California. The rotary is among the most amazing machines on the rails today, although their high cost of operation means that they are all too rarely seen in action.

A seemingly permanent fixture of the rail yard, a snowplow will sit immobile for months, sometimes years, waiting for the call to action. The plow is often the oldest piece of equipment on a railroad's roster. This classic, built by the Russell Snow Plow Co. of Ridgway, Pennsylvania, is owned by the Wisconsin Central.

Right
A Canadian Pacific plow clears the Lyndonville Subdivision at Barton, Vermont. Northern Vermont is notorious for its tough winter weather, as arctic storms blow down from Canada and dump lots of snow. This makes for good skiing, but difficult railroading. *Stephen D. Carlson*

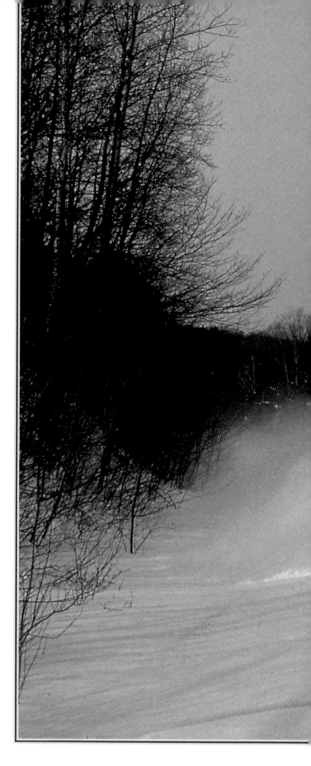

blade or "tongue," adjustable side-mounted wings, and a raised cupola for the plowmen to ride in. The plow is heavily weighted to minimize the likelihood of derailment when it is being shoved along through drifting snow at speeds up to 50 miles per hour. It's a fairly simple machine with minimal complicated equipment. A long air-actuated cylinder rides near the floor of the plow to raise and lower the front blade. Additional cylinders operate the hinged wings, which are used to give the plow additional covering power. These air-powered cylinders are essentially larger versions of the standard air-brake cylinders found on most conventional railway equipment, but instead of applying pressure to brake shoes, they move the tongue and wings. An auxiliary air reservoir fed by the main air-brake line serves these cylinders, which are controlled by the crew operating valves in the cupola. The crew monitors two gauges, one for the brake line and one for the auxiliary reservoir. Except for these basic controls, the cupola features few amenities.

The wedge plow is shoved along by conventional locomotives. On lines only lightly covered with snow, just one locomotive might be assigned to the plow, but in areas of heavy snow, it would be common to find two or three locomotives shoving a wedge plow. In the nineteenth century, as many as six to eight steam locomotives were assigned to Central Pacific's old Bucker snowplows working Donner Pass. The presence of the snowplow riding ahead of the locomotive, combined with the blinding effects of blowing and swirling snow, produces an awkward arrangement, as the engine crew shoving the plow cannot see where they are going. Instead, they must rely on the plow crew riding in the cupola to pilot them. The plow crew and the engine crew communicate as best they can. Traditionally this was done with whistle signals, but today they normally communicate on two-way radios, using whistle signals only in extreme circumstances.

As the plow races along, slicing through snow, shoving it forcefully to either side of the

This Lehigh Valley snowplow dates from an era when even the most utilitarian equipment was designed to look nice. Notice the wooden construction of the sides and wings. It was photographed on a snowless December day in 1971 at the Lehigh Valley yards at Sayre, Pennsylvania. *Doug Eisele*

tracks, the crew has to raise and lower the tongue and adjust the wings to clear obstructions on the line. The tongue must be lifted at highway grade crossings, track turnouts, and railway level crossings. Failure to lift the tongue at the appropriate time could cause the plow to derail and result in serious damage to the tracks and crossings. Railways mark all known obstructions along the line with clear warning signs that can be easily spotted in heavy snow. Different railways use a variety of different marking standards, and many types of signs or posts have been employed over the years.

Operating a snowplow requires great skill and nerves of steel. A plow crew has to be ready to take a call at any hour of the day in the very worst weather and, once called, must battle the elements for hours at a time. Plowmen must have detailed familiarity with the railway line they are working, knowing it backward, forward, and inside out. A stretch of track that you worked on all summer long looks very different when covered by several feet of blowing, drifting snow. With as much as 4,000 horsepower propelling you forward at up to 50 miles per hour, losing track of where you are can prove fatal. A single obstruction can easily derail the plow. At times, the snow can get too deep, such as in cuts where it

accumulates and drifts, or on mountainsides, where slides and avalanches can dump tons of snow on the tracks. This can cause a plow to bog down and stall. In most situations, the crew can back out and make a second run toward the obstruction, slamming into it with great force. It may take several runs to clear larger drifts.

Sometimes the plow derails. This can be very serious if the plow rolls over, but usually it's just inconvenient. Plowmen expect the inevitable derailment, and they typically carry a host of tools, such as rerailing "frogs," chains, jacks, and wrenches to assist with getting the plow back on the rails. Plowing is a dangerous job, but without the plows, the railway would shut down. Seeing a plow at work is like watching a rolling avalanche racing along, creating a storm of snow exploding forward as it clears the tracks, freeing the railway of its icy shackles.

Rotary Plows

The most significant nineteenth-century innovation in snow removal was the rotary snowplow. Wedge plows and locomotive pilot plows were adequate for clearing tracks in the East, where relatively moderate snowfall seasonally interrupted service. But as railways pushed westward across North America, crossing the Great Plains and surmounting high mountain passes where fantastic snow depths are common, these conventional plows proved lacking. The wedge plow—an effective tool for fighting small drifts and relatively light snow—suffers when put to the test in deep mountain snow. It is especially poor at clearing steeply graded lines, as the wedge plow needs to be shoved along at speed to be most effective. The railroads needed a way to combat the deep snow of mountain passes and quickly conquer snow slides and blockages.

On high western mountain passes, men waged war against nature, fighting to keep the tracks open in all weather. This was more than simply a matter of convenience; at times it was a matter of survival. In those days the railroad served as the lifeline to remote western communities, and without transportation, people were at risk of being cut off from civilization. Severe storms could shut down railways for days at a time. Railroads would employ every tool at their disposal to clear the line, often sending armies of men with snow shovels to dig through drifts and deep cuts clogged with snow.

The rotary plow was perfected during the mid-1880s, just in time to cope with some of the worst winter storms ever encountered: the terrible blizzards of 1887–1888, which remain legend to this day. The rotary is an amazing machine that was the brainchild of Canadian inventor Orange Jull. It was a tool whose time had come, and it arrived on the scene at just the right time. Jull derived his rotary plow from an earlier paddle plow designed by J. W. Eliot. Jull's prototype incorporated a pair of rotating fanlike blades spinning in opposite directions and powered by a stationary steam engine. The first set of blades fed snow into the plow, while the second set propelled the snow out through a chute.

Jull sold the manufacturing rights to his friends John and Edward Leslie. During the winter of 1883 and 1884, a prototype was constructed in Canada with the aid of the Canadian Pacific Railway. It was tested in the spring of 1884 and proved successful, generating some interest among the railways. The plow wasn't ready for general use, however, and over the next few years the Leslies refined Jull's design, implementing several significant improvements, and they went into business contracting the manufacturing of rotary plows. The Leslies did not actually assemble the rotary plows, and most were built at established locomotive manufacturing plants. Among the Leslies' improvements was a single simplified rotating fan that used a system of self-adjusting bladed cones to scoop and throw the snow. This was far more efficient than Jull's original double

This unusual-looking plow was built by the Boston & Maine in 1895. Photographed at the B&M yard in Northampton, Massachusetts, on April 9, 1934, it was stationed at East Deerfield the following winter, where it was assigned plowing duties north on the Connecticut River Line to East Northfield and on the Ashuelot and Turners Falls branches. *Photo by Donald Shaw, Robert A. Buck collection*

This double-track plow represents a different style of Boston & Maine plow. Like all plows from the period, it had no propulsion of its own and was shoved along by a steam locomotive. Built in Concord, New Hampshire, in 1904, this plow was stationed in the Boston area. It was photographed at B&M's Salem yard on January 26, 1936. *Donald Shaw, Robert A. Buck collection*

fan system. The Leslie fan was capable of moving more snow in less time, and it was less prone to breakdowns. They also added a reversible snow chute, which permitted snow to be directed to either side of the tracks. Lateral adjustable blades were employed to give the plow greater range by scooping snow from the sides of the tracks into the plow blades. Adjustable blades for ice cutting and flanging were used to minimize derailments and keep flangeways clear after the rotary fan had

cleared most of the heavy snow. By the 1890s, the basic steam rotary design had reached its common form. Later design improvements were a function of size, more modern construction materials, and finally the conversion of some plows to diesel-electric operation.

The Leslies were extremely successful with their snowplow enterprise, and sold many plows within just a few years. At first the western railroads were most interested in the rotary. The first 10 plows were all purchased by western lines and were quickly dispatched to clear the most difficult

mountain passes. The Union Pacific, Northern Pacific, Central Pacific, and Canadian Pacific all employed early rotaries, using them in the Blue Mountains of Oregon, Stampede Pass in Washington, over the California Sierra, and in the Canadian Rockies. Midwestern and snow-plagued eastern lines bought rotaries too, and the plow was eventually sold to railways around the world.

A rotary plow is an ominous looking machine, its great fan appearing like an enormous gaping mouth. A traditional rotary plow fan is powered by a stationary onboard reciprocating

Left

A Canadian Pacific plow train works at Wells River, Vermont, in March 1993. At one time a common sight in winter, these trains are becoming increasingly rare. Changes in railroading have led to far fewer branch lines, as well as more modern machinery and different service priorities. *Stephen D. Carlson*

The spinning blades of a rotary are designed to draw snow into the plow and blow it far from the tracks. Rotary plows are excellent tools for moving lots of wet heavy snow, which is why they are still used up on Donner Pass.

steam engine that operates on the same principle as the steam locomotive engine, using a firebox, boiler, and cylinders, except the engine is used strictly to turn the fan blades. (As explained earlier, the rotary is not a self-propelled machine and requires a conventional locomotive to push it along.) The steam engine turns a shaft, which is connected to beveled gears that turn the fan. The fan can rotate up to a maximum of 200 to 400 rpm, but normally works at approximately 90 rpm when blowing snow. The fan consists of conical scoops arranged in a hub and spoke network.

Each cone is fitted with self-adjusting hinged blades designed to feed snow into the cone as the plow moves along. The rapidly spinning conical blades scoop snow and by natural centrifugal forces thrust it out through the chute at the top of the plow. This system is especially efficient for rapidly clearing heavy wet snow, the variety commonly dumped in the western mountains.

The steam-powered rotary required a minimum of three men to operate it: an engineer and fireman to keep the engine running, and a pilot to guide the locomotive crew pushing the plow from behind. As in the case of a wedge plow, the locomotive crew pushing the plow is running blind, relying on the pilot's signals—traditionally a system of long and short whistles—to guide them. On mountainous lines, where grades exceed two

percent and snow depth might be greater than 10 feet, it was not unusual for several steam locomotives to push a single rotary.

The rotary plows were built in a variety of sizes. An early prototype was just 34 feet, 2 inches long; 12 feet, 8 inches high; and 9 feet, 6 inches wide. Its steam engine used a pair of double-acting 17x22 (bore and stroke) cylinders to develop an estimated 700 horsepower. Later plows used fans that ranged in circumference from 9 feet to more than 12 feet. The heaviest rotary weighed 150 tons, nearly five times more than the first. Cumbres & Toltec's former Rio Grande plows were among the smallest rotaries built. They had to accommodate the restrictive loading gauge of the Rio Grande's narrow-gauge line. The majority of steam-powered rotaries were erected by the American Locomotive Company (Alco) or its predecessors, and eventually Alco purchased the manufacturing rights from the Leslies, after the turn of the century.

Since the end of the steam era in the 1950s, rotaries have been largely supplanted by other,

Union Pacific rotary plow No. 900076 clears drifts at Bennett, Colorado, in March 1977. Diesel manufacturer Lima-Hamilton built this plow in December 1949, one of only four Leslie rotaries manufactured by L-H. *Jim Marcus, Doug Eisele collection*

A Southern Pacific flanger rests at Truckee, California, after a tough night clearing snow on Donner Pass. SP flangers made regular circuits between Truckee and Fulda to keep snow from accumulating on the tracks. Balloon tracks at both locations allow the flangers to reverse direction quickly without the locomotives needing to uncouple and run around.

more modern snowplows a result of the change from steam to diesel technology. Steam rotaries are expensive to maintain and operate, and diesels have made other plow designs more cost-effective. Despite this, some lines have held on to rotary plows, often converting them to diesel-electric operation. The Burlington was the first American line to make such a conversion, and Southern Pacific (SP), which operated the largest fleet of Leslie rotaries, successfully converted many of its plows and greatly prolonged their life (see "Rotary Encounter on Donner Pass" later in the chapter). Conversion to diesel-electric operation entails replacing the steam engine with traction motors and other electrical components and pairing the rotary with a diesel-electric engine to provide electric power. The great cost of converting a plow notwithstanding, the rotary design is more effective when electrically powered. SP's diesel-electric rotaries use four traction motors that generate up to 1,200 horsepower (almost twice the power of the early steam-powered prototypes) to turn the blades. Although rotaries are still used, their operation is infrequent at best, and sometimes years pass between runs.

The Cumbres & Toltec Scenic, which operates a 64-mile-long narrow-gauge line in Colorado and New Mexico (one of the last remnants of the Denver & Rio Grande Western narrow-gauge empire), still uses a steam rotary to clear its line. The western slope of Cumbres Pass is a tortuous 4 percent climb, cresting at just over 10,000 feet above sea level. As many as three 2-8-2 Mikados are required to shove the plow when clearing this line.

Jull Centrifugal Excavator

Despite the success of his rotary plow invention, Orange Jull was dissatisfied with his arrangement with the Leslie brothers. In frustration, he invented another snowplow that carried his name: the Jull Centrifugal Excavator. It used an enormous steam-powered angled auger to propel snow, in an arrangement similar to that employed today on many home-use snow blowers. While the design was effective and generated some interest among American railways, it didn't work as well as the rotary. Jull received only a handful of orders for his Excavator. Today the Excavator is little more than an historical curiosity, whereas the Leslie rotary plow had a 60-year production run and still can be seen in use today.

Flangers and Spreaders

More common than the rotary plow for modern snow removal are flangers and spreaders. Spreaders are typically used to move moderate

In the heavy snows near Donner Pass, Jordan Spreaders and rotary plows work in tandem to keep the double-track lines clear. On February 22, 1993, the Jordan is working eastbound on the No. 1 track toward Soda Springs. It dumps the snow into the path of a rotary plow, which will follow a few minutes later on the No. 2 track.

Southern Pacific's Leslie rotary plow clears the No. 2 main track west of Soda Springs, California. Donner Pass is one of the Leslie rotary's last remaining stomping grounds.

amounts of snow; flangers keep a line open in areas of heavy snowfall. Flangers are pulled along by conventional diesel locomotives that are equipped for snow service and have electrical controls to operate the flanger blades from the locomotive cab. The flanger itself has a body somewhat narrower than that of a conventional railway car. It has two blades that can be lowered below rail level to clear snow and ice accumula-

Electrified railroads have special plowing considerations. Metro-North has to make sure its electric third rail is kept free of snow and ice. On January 6, 2001, an RM-700 snow blower clears snow at Katonah, New York, on the old New York Central Harlem Division. *Patrick Yough*

tion on the tracks and keep the flangeways open. Clearing the flangeway is the most important function of a flanger. The wheel flange is what guides a railway car and holds the train on the tracks, and ice-clogged flangeways can derail a train. The flanger operator can direct the snow to either the left or right side of the tracks, and raise and lower the blades to avoid obstructions in the same way that a wedge plow operator controls the plow tongue. A flanger might run at 35 to 40 miles per hour, as its effectiveness is, in part, a function of speed. While a flanger is an excellent tool for keeping a line open, if snow continues to accumulate, a railway will need to call on more powerful equipment to clear the tracks.

Southern Pacific routinely maintained five flanger sets at its yards in Roseville, California, to keep its extremely snowy Donner Pass crossing open. In modern times, SP powered its flanger sets

A Burlington Northern snow blower clears the Hoffmans Avenue interlocking at Dayton's Bluff in St. Paul, Minnesota, on January 19, 1994. This type of equipment is often used to keep switches from becoming clogged with snow and ice.

with specially equipped Electro-Motive Division SD9's or, in SP's last years, with snow-service GP38-2s. These locomotives worked regular freight duties in the off-season. To keep the flanger sets moving and to minimize turning time and delays to trains on the mainline, SP constructed special "balloon tracks," or loops, at key locations. SP also regularly assigned flangers to its other snowy mountain crossings, including Pengra Pass in the Oregon Cascades and Siskiyou Summit near Ashland, Oregon.

Another common snow-fighting tool is a Jordan Spreader adapted for snow service. Many railways adopted snow-service Jordans instead of relying on the more traditional railway plows such as rotaries and Russell wedge plows. The basic configuration of a Jordan Spreader, equipped with an adjustable front-end plow and large hinged wings, is well suited to heavy snow removal. The front-end plow clears the snow off the tracks and can be arranged to push the snow to either side. The Jordan's extendable wings are used to plow snow well beyond the normal width of the tracks that the spreader is running on. This allows the Jordan to clear a double-Track mainline, or to move large amounts of snow well clear of the tracks. A Jordan is suited for diesel-electric operations, and as in the case of other traditional plow types, it can be shoved by one or more diesels in order to move heavy snow. Diesel locomotives offered a big improvement for snow plowing, since a diesel can produce maximum power at slow speeds, while a steam locomotive cannot.

In the 1960s, Southern Pacific ordered two specially designed spreaders for its Donner Pass route, and these are among the largest of the type. According to Dick Dorn in his December 1994 article in *Trains* magazine, SP's big snow-service Jordans can move as much as 125,000 pounds of snow per second when traveling at speed with wings fully extended. The advent of these spreaders reduced SP's reliance on its famous rotary plows, as the spreaders are fully capable of handling all but the worst snow conditions.

Modern Snow-Fighting Machines

Railways are expected to operate 24 hours a day, regardless of weather. While the antique plows of nineteenth century design are used to clear the railway in extreme situations, many railways operating in snowy climates have other tools for keeping their lines clear during lighter snowfall. Even light snow clogs switch points, fouls junctions, yards, and terminals, making day-to-day operations difficult, so railways rely on switch-point heaters, snow blowers, snow jets, and other equipment to keep daily operations fluid.

Today, many lines dispatch trains remotely, using computerized centralized traffic control (CTC) to authorize train movements and set switches. Union Pacific directs its trains from Omaha, Nebraska; CSX from Jacksonville, Florida; and Burlington Northern Santa Fe from Fort Worth, Texas. So a dispatcher sitting in a comfortable climate-controlled dispatch center, a thousand miles from the route he's responsible for, will be lining a route with his computer mouse, as snow slowly covers the tracks. In order to minimize the difficulties with remote-controlled switch operation, many dispatcher-controlled sidings and junctions are equipped with switch-point heaters or blowers to keep points from icing up and ensure that the switches operate properly.

The Leslie rotary snow plow is the ultimate snow-fighting machine, but it takes a heavy winter snow, like the one that fell on Emigrant Gap near Donner Pass in February 1993, to bring these venerable machines out for the job.

In the blue glow of evening on February 23, 1993,
a Southern Pacific snow-service Jordan Spreader emerges from the west portal of Tunnel 6 at Donner Pass. The Jordan Spreader proved an effective snow removal machine in most situations, relegating the rotary plows to only the most difficult work.

Some remote switch-point heaters are fitted with sophisticated snow-detection monitors that turn the heaters on and off as conditions change, while others rely on railroad workers to operate them manually. It is important to run switch heaters only when ice and snow are accumulating, and not when it's just raining. Several companies manufacture snow-detection equipment to deal with

these needs. The Rails Company sells an electro-optical detection system that employs microprocessor-controlled sensors to distinguish between different types of precipitation. Spectrum Infrared offers an infrared detection system.

To clear switches in yards and at junctions, railroads employ snow blowers and snow jets. Harsco's Fairmont Tamper division builds a Typhoon snow blower designed to clear switches. This self-propelled machine uses a hydraulically powered centrifugal fan to blast air downward at speeds up to 160 miles per hour, and a heavy-duty scarifying broom. A far more powerful snow removal tool is the snow jet, which uses a jet engine to blast snow from the track. One of the pioneers of the snow jet was New York Central, which operated many of its largest yards in the Great Lakes Snow Belt where lake-effect snow can paralyze operations for days. It constructed several snow jets at its company shops in the 1960s, using surplus jet engines. The jet engine rides on a self-propelled platform powered by a small diesel engine with a hydraulic transmission. Central's snow jet can run up to 20 miles per hour when not blowing snow, but when it is blowing snow it moves much slower. The jet thrusts hot air at 65,000 pounds downward, blowing and melting snow. The air temperature ranges between 200 and 300 degrees Fahrenheit, but it is the force of the air, rather than the heat, that is primarily responsible for removing snow. Even with this great force, crews typically make at least two passes over each switch to ensure it is free of obstructing ice and snow. The snow jets have been working for more than 30 years for New York Central and its successors Penn Central, Conrail, and now CSX.

Today, many lines regularly use snow jets to clear yard switches, and they can be purchased commercially from Essco. The modern Essco Snowjet is diesel-hydraulic powered, allowing travel speeds of up to 30 miles per hour, and it features a rotating jet nozzle.

Railways also use less specialized tools for snow removal as well. Ballast regulators and bulldozers are often equipped for snow service. Although far less spectacular, and not capable of moving the great quantities of snow of traditional plows, these modern machines require far less labor than the older plows, allowing railroads to keep winter employment costs down. Typically only one man is needed to operate a ballast regulator in snow service, compared to a crew of six for a typical Russell plow set. Still, when the big storms hit, the old plows still find their day in the snow!

A working Leslie rotary snowplow is an amazing piece of railway equipment, but it is among the most elusive. Finding one in action on a mainline is one of the greatest challenges a railway photographer can undertake. A rotary is labor-intensive and expensive to operate, and as a result it is called upon only after all other means of snow removal have been exhausted. During the early 1990s, I spent several winters photographing Southern Pacific's rugged Donner Pass crossing in the Sierra Nevada of California—a place legendary for its heavy snowfall. But even here, in one of the last regular domains of the Leslie Rotary, drought conditions prevailed for the better part of a decade, and while heavy snow fell at times, Southern Pacific largely relied on its fleet of flangers, spreaders, and contract bulldozers to keep Donner open to traffic.

Southern Pacific's mainline over Donner Pass was completed in 1868 by SP's predecessor, Central Pacific, as the western portion of the original transcontinental railroad, famous for its legendary joining at Promontory, Utah, on May 10, 1869. This amazing mountain crossing is one of the most famous in American railroading. It was the vision of western railroad pioneer Theodore Judah, who personally surveyed much of the route, gathered California businessmen to raise the capital needed to build the railroad, and lobbied Congress and the resident to pass the necessary legislation—but Judah never lived to see the route completed. The railroad climbs out of the Central Valley at an elevation just above sea level to the summit of the Sierra at Donner Pass, ascending to more than 7,000 feet above sea level in just 90 miles. In so doing, the route passes directly through one of the heaviest snowfall regions in the Continental United States. In a light year, more than 200 inches of snow will fall at Donner; in a heavy one, more than 800 inches.

As California grew, traffic over Donner boomed. A second track was completed over the route in October 1925, and during World War II the railroad was handling as many as 100 moves a day. After the war, however, this once-crucial thoroughfare entered a long period of decline. By the early 1990s, though the Donner Pass crossing was still functioning as a primary mainline between California and the East, hosting a dozen freights and Amtrak's Chicago-Oakland *California Zephyr* every day, it had lost its predominant role as

Rotary Encounter On Donner Pass

the way west. Other railway routes were busier, and Interstate 80, which runs parallel to the railroad over Donner, became the main artery to northern California.

The long drought subsided during the winter of 1992–1993, and a wave of fierce Pacific storms pounded California, bringing badly needed rain to low areas and heavy snow to higher elevations. By early February 1993, roughly 10 feet of snow had fallen at Donner Pass, and Southern Pacific was running out of places to put it. Then a new series of storms dumped more heavy snow on the Sierra, and the conditions were set for SP to call out its Leslies. This was my opportunity to catch the big plows in action! I carefully watched the weather, waiting for my chance. My friend and fellow photographer Brian Jennison lived at the foot of the Sierra's east slope near Reno, Nevada. When I called him on the evening of February 21 for a status report, he replied, "Hey kid, if you want the rotaries, get up here tonight. They're already out of Roseville [California] and have an early morning call out of the Gap [Emigrant Gap on Donner's west slope] for the run over the mountain to Truckee."

Wasting no time, I flew to Reno, where my Toyota pickup was waiting. In the early hours of February 22, I chained up my truck, donned my winter gear, and fought my way over Donner, reaching Emigrant Gap just as SP crews were preparing a set of rotaries for the trip over the mountain. Beasts of another era, the rotaries are among the last working remnants of the steam age. Though SP's plows had long since been converted to diesel-electric operation, they still retained a steam-era appearance. Steam wisped from their blades, keeping them free of snow accumulation.

At Emigrant Gap the snow was only a few feet deep, but at Norden, near the summit, there was an accumulated snowpack about 17 feet deep. Despite a long historical precedent, this plowing of Donner was far from a routine exercise, as it had been eight years since the last rotary plow had cleared the pass. I was among several photographers that day who had dropped everything to record the event.

The rotary set consisted of two plows, each coupled to a specially converted Electro-Motive Division F7 B-unit (cabless locomotive) to power the rotary blades, with four of SP's big Electro-Motive Division "tunnel motor" diesel-electric locomotives to propel the plows over the mountain. This was two more locomotives than SP traditionally used to power its rotary plows, but the railroad was not taking any chances. Preceding the rotary-set up the mountain was one of SP's specially designed Jordan Spreaders, which ran on the opposite track to plow snow into the path of the rotary. The rotary would follow close behind and blow the snow far from the tracks. Soon this procession of men and machines was under way and working up the mountain. I set up at Yuba Pass, a few miles from Emigrant Gap, and made my first photograph of the mighty plows in action. Over the next few days, I had numerous opportunities to catch these fantastic machines in action, and the results are displayed in this book.

The second day of plowing began at Truckee, California. The plows had cleared the lower of the two Donner crossings the day before, but the original crossing, which followed a different alignment, had been closed to traffic as a result of the heavy snow. While the lower crossing utilized a 2-mile-long tunnel, the original line was more circuitous, employing a series of shorter tunnels and snowsheds while skirting the north face of Mt. Judah (named for the line's surveyor). Drifts and piles of snow, some more than 10 feet deep, covered the tracks. SP hoped its legendary rotaries could reopen this difficult mountain crossing. Brian Jennison and I set out toward Truckee to intercept the rotaries on

their westward run over Donner. In the winter, there is little highway access to the tracks, as most of the trails used in drier months are buried under many feet of snow. This greatly limited where we could shoot the plows from. Furthermore, our arrival at Truckee was delayed by a serious snow-related accident on I-80; two trucks had crashed, blocking the westbound lanes for an hour. Despite these difficulties, we made it to Truckee in time to catch the plows leaving. We then drove to the summit, where we hoped to catch them clearing the "Chinese Wall," that section of track riding high on a man-made shelf cut into the rock face of Mt. Judah between two snowsheds. Plowing was very slow that day as the rotaries fought their way through Coldstream Canyon on their way up Donner Pass. We never got the shot of the rotaries crossing the Chinese Wall, because the plows derailed when they encountered an enormous drift on the closed line. Even the mightiest of snowplows are sometimes defeated. SP eventually got the line open, and the rotaries returned to Roseville, mission completed. This turned out to be the final winter for the original 1868 crossing. In the summer of 1993, cost-conscious SP discontinued operations over the older route, choosing to rely exclusively on its newer crossing.

Having witnessed a multitude of railway operations around the world, I can say with certainty that seeing SP's rotaries in action was one of the most impressive sights in all of railroading, and definitely one of the rarest!

"We've scored the rotaries, kid!" exclaimed Brian Jennison on exposing his first frame of Kodachrome at Truckee, California, in February 1993. On the moning of February 23, after battling snarled traffic on I-80, we finally made it to Truckee to find the rotaries in all their glory, steaming and ready to assault the east slope of Donner Pass. It was still snowing hard, and visibility was poor. Later in the day these plows derailed on the No. 1 track at the summit.

Index

Other titles by this author that you might enjoy include:

Locomotive
ISBN: 0-7603-0996-5

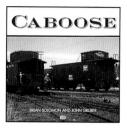

Caboose
ISBN: 0-7603-0895-0

Bullet Trains
ISBN: 0-7603-0768-7

**Narrow Gauge
Steam Locomotives**
ISBN: 0-7603-0543-9

Super Steam Locomotives
ISBN: 0-7603-0757-1

American Steam Locomotive
ISBN: 0-7603-0336-3

**The American
Diesel Locomotive**
ISBN: 0-7603-0666-4